ETHICS
An Outline

Benedict Spinoza

Edited by

Maja Trochimczyk

Series

Classic Wisdom

No. 2

ETHICS

DEMONSTRATED IN GEOMETRICAL ORDER AND DIVIDED INTO FIVE PARTS

WHICH TREAT

I. OF GOD
II. OF THE NATURE AND ORIGIN OF THE MIND,
III. OF THE ORIGIN AND NATURE OF THE AFFECTS.
IV. OF HUMAN BONDAGE, OR OF THE STRENGTH OF THE AFFECTS.
V. OF THE POWER OF THE INTELLECT, OR OF HUMAN LIBERTY.

BY

BENEDICT SPINOZA

Translated from the Latin

BY

WILLIAM HALE WHITE & MAJA TROCHIMCZYK

LOS ANGELES:
MOONRISE PRESS, 2017

Copyright Page

Ethics: An Outline by Benedict Spinoza, translated by William Hale White and Maja Trochimczyk

This book is a publication of Moonrise Press P.O. Box 4288, Los Angeles – Sunland, CA 91041-4288

© Copyright 2017 by Moonrise Press for cover design, preface, editing, and layout. The text of *Ethica Ordine Geometrico Demonstrata* by Benedict de Spinoza (Baruch Spinoza, 1632-1677) first published in 1677, is in public domain, and so is the translation by William Hale White (1831-1913), first published in 1883. The edited version contains about half of the original text and gender-neutral language.

All Rights Reserved to this version only.

While the content is the public domain, its layout, pagination and index are under copyright. No part of this book may be reproduced or utilized in any form or by any means, electronic or mechanical, including photocopying and recording, or by any information storage and retrieval system, without permission in writing from the publisher.

Book design and layout by Maja Trochimczyk using fonts: Cambria and Times Roman. Cover design by Maja Trochimczyk with a photograph by Maja Trochimczyk.

This is the second volume in a reprint series, Classic Wisdom.

MANUFACTURED IN THE UNITED STATES OF AMERICA

The Library of Congress Publication Data:

Benedict Spinoza (1632-1677) translated by William Hale White (1831-1913), edited by Maja Trochimczyk (b. 1957)

Ethics: An Outline. Pp. xii + 140 (162 total pages), 15.2 x 22.9 cm.

ISBN 978-1-945938-08-5 (paperback)
ISBN 978-1-945938-09-2 (eBook – EPUB format)

ETHIC

DEMONSTRATED IN GEOMETRICAL ORDER AND DIVIDED INTO FIVE PARTS,

WHICH TREAT

I. OF GOD.
II. OF THE NATURE AND ORIGIN OF THE MIND.
III. OF THE ORIGIN AND NATURE OF THE AFFECTS.
IV. OF HUMAN BONDAGE, OR OF THE STRENGTH OF THE AFFECTS.
V. OF THE POWER OF THE INTELLECT, OR OF HUMAN LIBERTY.

BY

BENEDICT DE SPINOZA.

Translated from the Latin

BY

WILLIAM HALE WHITE.

LONDON:
TRÜBNER & CO., LUDGATE HILL.
1883.
[All rights reserved.]

CONTENTS

- Why an Outline? Maja Trochimczyk ≡ vii
- Abbreviations and Latin Translations ≡ x

- **AN OUTLINE OF ETHICS ≡ 1**

- First Part: Of God ≡ 3
- Second Part:
  Of The Nature and Origin of The Mind ≡ 19
- Third Part:
  Of The Origin and Nature of the Affects ≡ 42
- Fourth Part:
  Of Human Bondage, or of the Strength of the Affects ≡ 81
- Fifth Part:
  Of The Power of the Intellect, Or of Human Liberty ≡ 121

WHY AN OUTLINE?

The more things change, the more they stay the same. After taking a philosophy class way back in college and not caring one way or another for Spinoza whose geometric way of presenting his philosophical, religious, ethical, ontological and epistemological views did not appeal to me at all, I finally discovered his immensely significant, timeless wisdom and decided to share it by reprinting the Ethics in an 19th-century English translation by William Hale White, in convenient paperback and EBook formats. This is the first in our new reprint series, Classic Wisdom. This wisdom is evident starting right in the first Part, on God:

> "PROP. XI. — God or substance consisting of infinite attributes, each one of which expresses eternal and infinite essence necessarily exists. PROP. XV. — Whatever is, is in God, and nothing can either be or be conceived without God."

Thus, God by virtue of being infinite, cannot be outside of this world (transcendental), God has to be and is immanent, God is in everything that exists. Everything that exists is in God, i.e., Divine. This, of course, is a path straight to the modern understanding of the united Universe, permeated by the creative energy of its Source, the One Divine Being that is all in all. This of course, is not compatible with the dogmas and teachings of any temple or church that separate the One into Many, or cut-off the Divine Spirit from matter. What an amazing revolution, hidden in plain sight! To obfuscate things, Spinoza's theories have been called "Philosophical Monism," "Pantheistic" or "Rationalist" and engendering ideas that gave the birth to Enlightenment.

Born in a Sephardic Jewish-Portuguese community in Amsterdam in 1621 (his ancestors excepted the Inquisition), he was expelled from the Jewish community at 23 years old, and is buried in the courtyard of a Christian Nieuwe Kerk in The Hague (he died at 44 years old in 1677). He was neither Jewish nor Christian in his views, and, from today's perspective may be called one of the early Classics of Awakened

Wisdom: the awakening is to the intrinsic unity of all that exist with God, the immortality of the human spirit, and the primacy of Love over all, Divine Light and Love guiding humans along their individual paths towards awakening, increased awareness and wisdom.

Philosophers love Spinoza for the elegance of his writings and the depth of his logical analysis of theorems and dogmas that he, time after time, proves absurd. The book consists of five parts: I. Of God; II. Of The Nature and Origin of the Mind, III. Of The Origin and Nature of the Affects; IV. Of Human Bondage, or of the Strength of the Affects. And V. Of The Power of the Intellect, or Of Human Liberty.

Just like the ancient Gnostics, Pythagoras, Plotinus, Hermes Trismegistos (many who wrote under his name), Giordano Bruno, and, to skip half a millennium, modern deep ecologists (Arne Dekke Eide Næss, and James Lovelock of the Gaia hypothesis), Spinoza found and shared the unified understanding of nature, humanity and divinity that dispels darkness, sorrows and doubts, while crowning the human being with the unperishable Divine Light that exists within. As he said: "The affect of Joy and its offspring increases the perfection of the mind and therefore is good; the affect of Sorrow and its offspring decreases the perfection of the mind and therefore is not good." Thus, to seek Joy and intellectual Love that unites the seeker with the Divine is the ultimate goal of human life.

This idea reminds casual readers of the recently popular "The Secret" teaching millions about the power of positive thinking, based on a premise that the "Universe" gives the individual an exact response to what that person thinks or feels like – the haters will be hated back and hurt, the lovers will be loved, the fearful – scared, and the joyous will have a lot more to en joy. Who knows how it really works, but there are many things worth doing less than reading Spinoza.

For convenience of those who did not grow up studying Latin, we added Arab numerals to the Propositions and other numbered lists. We also added more paragraph breaks to make the text easier to follow on the page. The index, due to changed pagination, had to be redone, only the main entries were preserved, and additional items added. Finally, the title was changed to plural, Ethics, not Ethic as White had it, following the original.

Spinoza's wisdom will reach you if you are patient and read this volume with a discerning mind. In this abbreviated vversion, we took out most of the scholastic arguments about the nature and attributes of God, substances, and the like. Instead, we kept all the conclusions and lessons about ethical living, affection, and virtues, because of their practical applications.

For practical use as a guide to ethical life, the demonstrations and arguments why the Propositions are true are not needed. But it is important to easily number and find them, as well as to be able to read it and apply to a personal life, whether the reader is a man or a woman.
In accordance with the principles of gender-neutral language that does not discriminate against women, the use of "man/men" was replaced with "human being," "person" and "people" throughout. Similarly, since God in Spinoza's concept is not a male, the pronouns *He* and *His* have been replaced throughout by *God* and *God's* respectively. This infinite, eternal Being that is immanent in the Universe is the same Being as that known in Awakened circles as Father-Mother-God, or Source, or the One. The use of just the word "God" is more convenient in this case.

This summary of Spinoza's Ethics is for practical use – and the reduced amount of text is designed for easier reading and absorption of the main ideas.

Enjoy!

~ *Maja Trochimczyk*

ABBREVIATIONS

- Ax. ≡ Axiom
- Corol. ≡ Corollary
- Def. ≡ Definition
- Demonst. ≡ Demonstration
- Q.E.D. ≡ *Quod Erat Demonstrandum*, what was to be demonstrated (Latin), or, for physics students, *Quite Easily Done*
- Pt. ≡ Part
- Post. ≡ Postulate
- Prop. ≡ Proposition
- Schol. ≡ Scholium
- &c. ≡ Et Cetera

LATIN QUOTATIONS

The following expressions appear in Latin in the text:

- *anima pathema* ≡ Affect
- *animositas* ≡ strength of mind
- *ad infinitum* ≡ again and again, forever
- *a priori* ≡ from the earlier, theoretical knowledge
- *a posteriori* ≡ from the latter, experiential knowledge
- *cum suo ideato (Lat.)* ≡ with its idea
- *denominationes intrinsecas* ≡ intrinsic denomination, referring to a things own's properties
- *finem indigentice et finem assimilationis* ≡ the end of want and the end of assimilation
- *reductio ad absurdum* ≡ reduce to absurdity, logical argument to show the fallacy of a thesis
- *reductio ad ignorantiam* ≡ argument from ignorance, a logical argument to show the fallacy of a thesis
- *rem cogitantem* ≡ the thinking thing (i.e. intellectual)
- *rem extensam* ≡ the extended thing (i.e. physical)
- *idea Dei* ≡ the idea of God (or God's idea)

- *Speremus pariter, pariter metuamus amantes; Ferreus est, aliquis, quod sinit alter, amat.* [≡ Ferreus est, aliquis, quod sinit alter, amat. ... Speremus pariter, pariter metuamus amantes] ≡ Let us hope that while we fear lovers, one is strong and allows the other in love; a quotation from Ovid's *Amores,* Liber secundus, XIX, with the order of phrases changed by Spinoza
- *secundum fieri,* or, *causalitas / causa secundum fieri* ≡ causality with respect to becoming (coming into being), a medieval scholastic term
- *secundum esse,* or, *causalitas / causa secundum esse* ≡ causality with respect to being, a medieval scholastic term.
- *Video proboque, deteriora sequor* ≡ I see the better way and approve it, but I follow the worse way, a Latin proverb
- *Vice versa* ≡ the other way around

ETHICS: AN OUTLINE

First Part

OF GOD

DEFINITIONS

I. By **cause of itself,** I understand that, whose essence involves existence; or that, whose nature cannot be conceived unless existing.

II. That thing is called **finite in its own kind** (*in suo genere*) which can be limited by another thing of the same nature. For example, a body is called finite, because we always conceive another which is greater. So a thought is limited by another thought; but a body is not limited by a thought, nor a thought by a body.

IIL By **substance,** I understand that which is in itself and is conceived through itself; in other words, that, the conception of which does not need the conception of another thing from which it must be formed.

IV. By **attribute**, I understand that which the intellect perceives of substance, as if constituting its essence.

V. By **mode,** I understand the affections of substance, or that which is in another thing through which also it is conceived.

VI. By **God,** I understand Being absolutely infinite, that is to say, substance consisting of infinite attributes, each one of which expresses eternal and infinite essence.

Explanation. — I say absolutely infinite but not infinite in its own kind (*in suo genere*); for of whatever is infinite only in its own kind (*in suo genere*), we can deny infinite attributes; but to the essence of that which is absolutely infinite pertains whatever expresses essence and involves no negation.

VII. That thing is called **free** which exists from the necessity of its own nature alone, and is determined to action by itself alone. That thing, on the other hand, is called necessary, or rather compelled, which by another is determined to existence and action in a fixed and prescribed manner.

VIII. By **eternity,** I understand existence itself, so far as it is conceived necessarily to follow from the definition alone of an eternal thing.

Explanation. — For such an existence is conceived as eternal truth; and also as the essence of the thing. It cannot therefore be explained by duration or time, even if the duration be conceived without beginning or end.

AXIOMS

I. Everything which is, is either in itself or in another.

II. That which cannot be conceived through another must be conceived through itself.

III. From a given determinate cause an effect necessarily follows; and, on the other hand, if no determinate cause be given, it is impossible that an effect can follow.

IV. The knowledge (*cognitio*) of an effect depends upon and involves the knowledge of the cause.

V. Those things which have nothing mutually in common with one another cannot through one another be mutually understood, that is to say, the conception of the one does not involve the conception of the other.

VI. A true idea must agree with that of which it is the idea (*cum suo ideato*).

VII. The essence of that thing which can be conceived as not existing does not involve existence.

OF GOD

PROP. 1. — *Substance is by its nature prior to its affections.*

PROP. 2. — *Two substances having different attributes have nothing in common with one another.*

PROP. 3. — *If two things have nothing in common with one another, one cannot be the cause of the other.*

PROP. 4. — *Two or more distinct things are distinguished from one another, either by the difference of the attributes of the substances, or by the difference of their affections.*

PROP. 5. — *In nature there cannot be two or more substances of the same nature or attribute.*

PROP. 6. — *One substance cannot be produced by another substance.*

PROP. 7. — *It pertains to the nature of substance to exist.*

PROP. 8. — *Every substance is necessarily infinite.*

PROP. 9. — *The more reality or being a thing possesses, the more attributes belong to it.*

PROP. 10. — *Each attribute of a substance must be conceived through itself.*

PROP. 11. — *God or substance consisting of infinite attributes, each one of which expresses eternal and infinite essence necessarily exists.*

PROP. 12. — *No attribute of substance can be truly conceived from which it follows that substance can be divided.*

PROP. 13. — *Substance absolutely infinite is indivisible.*

PROP. 14. — *Besides God, no substance can be nor can be conceived.*

Hence it follows with the greatest clearness, firstly, that God is one, that is to say (Def. 6), in nature there is but one substance, and it is absolutely infinite.

It follows, secondly, that the thing extended *(rem extensam)* and the thing thinking *(rem cogitantem)* are either attributes of God or (Ax. 1) affections of the attributes of God.

PROP. 15. — *Whatever is, is in God, and nothing can either be or be conceived without God.*

There are those who imagine God to be like a human being, composed of body and soul and subject to passions; but it is clear enough from what has already been demonstrated how far off people who believe this are from the true knowledge of God. But these I dismiss, for all people who have in any way looked into the divine nature deny that God is corporeal. That God cannot be so they conclusively prove by showing that by "body" we understand a certain quantity possessing length, breadth, and depth, limited by some fixed form; and that to attribute these to God, a being absolutely infinite, is the greatest absurdity.

Outside God no substance can exist from which the divine nature could suffer. All things, I say, are in God, and everything which takes place takes place by the laws alone of the infinite nature of God, and follows from the necessity of God's essence.

Therefore in no way whatever can it be asserted that God suffers from anything, or that substance extended, even if it be supposed divisible, is unworthy of the divine nature, provided only it be allowed that it is eternal and infinite.

PROP. 16. — *From the necessity of the divine nature infinite numbers of things in infinite ways {that is to say, all things which can be conceived by the infinite intellect} must follow.*

Corol. 1. — Hence it follows that God is the efficient cause of all things which can fall under the infinite intellect.

Corol. 2. — It follows, secondly, that God is cause through Godself, and not through that which is contingent (*per accidens*).

Corol. 3. — It follows, thirdly, that God is absolutely the first cause.

PROP. 17. — *God acts from the laws of God's own nature only, and is compelled by no one.*

Corol. 1. — Hence it follows, firstly, that there is no cause, either external to God or within God, which can excite God to act except. the perfection of God's own nature.

Corol. 2. — It follows, secondly, that God alone is a free cause; for God alone exists from the necessity alone of God's own nature , and acts from the necessity alone of God's own nature. Therefore, God alone is a free cause. .

PROP. 18. — *God is the immanent, and not the transitive cause of all things.*

All things which are, are in God and must be conceived through God, and therefore God is the cause of the things which are in Godself. This is the first thing which was to be proved. Moreover, outside God there can be no substance, that is to say, outside God nothing can exist which is in itself.

PROP. 19. — *God is eternal, or, in other words, all God's attributes are eternal.*

PROP. 20. — *The existence of God and God's essence are one and the same thing.*

Corol. 1. — Hence it follows, 1. That the existence of God, like God's essence, is an eternal truth.

Corol. 2. — It follows, 2. That God is immutable, or (which is the same thing) all God's attributes are immutable; for if they were changed as regards their existence, they must be changed also as regards their essence; that is to say (as is self-evident), from being true, they would become false, which is absurd.

PROP. 21. — *All things which follow from the absolute nature of any attribute of God must forever exist, and must be infinite; that is to say, through that same attribute they are eternal and infinite.*

PROP. 22. — *Whatever follows from any attribute of God, in so far as it is modified by a modification, which through the same attribute exists necessarily and infinitely, must also exist necessarily and infinitely.*

PROP. 23. — *Every mode which exists necessarily and infinitely must necessarily follow either from the absolute nature of some attribute of God, or from some attribute modified by a modification which exists necessarily and infinitely.*

PROP. 24. — *The essence of things produced by God does not involve existence.*

Corol.— Hence it follows that God is not only the cause of the commencement of the existence of things, but also of their continuance in existence, or, in other words (to use scholastic phraseology), God is the *causa essendi rerum*. For if we consider the essence of things, whether existing or non-existing, we discover that it neither involves existence nor duration, and therefore the essence of existing things cannot be the cause of their existence nor of their duration, but God only is the cause, to whose nature alone existence pertains.

PROP. 25. — *God is not only the efficient cause of the existence of things, but also of their essence.*

Corol.— Individual things are nothing but affections or modes of God's attributes, expressing those attributes in a certain and determinate manner.

PROP. 26. — *A thing which has been determined to any action was necessarily so determined by God, and that which has not been thus determined by God cannot determine itself to action.*

PROP. 27. — *A thing which has been determined by God to any action cannot render itself indeterminate.*

PROP. 28. — *An individual thing, or a thing which is finite and which has a determinate existence, cannot exist nor be determined to action unless it be determined to existence and action by another cause which is also finite and has a determinate existence; and again, this cause cannot exist nor be determined to action unless by another cause which is also finite and determined to existence and auction, and so on* ad infinitum.

Schol. — Since certain things must have been immediately produced by God, that is to say, those which necessarily follow from God's absolute nature; these primary products being the mediating ca use for those things which, nevertheless, without God can neither be nor can be conceived; it follows, firstly, that of things immediately produced by God. God is the proximate cause absolutely, and not in their own kind (*in suo genere*), as we say; for effects of God can neither be nor be conceived without their cause.

It follows, secondly, that God cannot be properly called the remote cause of individual things, unless for the sake of distinguishing them from the things which God has immediately produced, or rather which follow from God's absolute nature. For by a remote cause we understand that which is in no way joined to its effect. But all things which are, are in God, and so depend upon God that without God they can neither be nor be conceived.

PROP. 29. — *In nature there is nothing contingent, but all things are determined from the necessity of the divine nature to exist and act in a certain manner.*

Schol.— Before I go any farther, I wish here to explain, or rather to recall to recollection, what we mean by *natura naturans* and what by *natura naturata*.[1] For, from what has gone before, I think it is plain that by *natura naturans* we are to understand that which is in itself and is conceived through itself, or those attributes of

---

[1] These are two expressions derived from a scholastic philosophy which strove to signify by the same verb the oneness of God and the world, and yet at the same time to mark by a difference of inflexion the same that there was not absolute identity, — Tr.

substance which express eternal and infinite essence, that is to say, God in so far as God is considered as a free cause. But by *natura naturata* I understand everything which follows from the necessity of the nature of God, or of any one of God's attributes, that is to say, all the modes of God's attributes in so far as they are considered as things which are in God, and which without God can neither be nor can be conceived.

PROP. 30. — *The actual intellect, whether finite or infinite, must comprehend the attributes of God and the affections of God, and nothing else.*

PROP. 31. — *The actual intellect, whether it be finite or infinite, together with the will, desire, love, &c., must be referred to the* natura naturata *and not to the* natura naturans.

Schol. — I do not here speak of the actual intellect because I admit that any intellect potentially exists, but because I wish, in order that there may be no confusion, to speak of nothing excepting of that which we perceive with the utmost clearness, that is to say, the understanding itself, which we perceive as clearly as we perceive anything. For we can understand nothing through the intellect which does not lead to a more perfect knowledge of the understanding.

PROP. 32. — *The will cannot be called a free cause, but can only be called necessary.*

Corol. 1. — Hence it follows, firstly, that God does not act from freedom of the will.

Corol. 2. — It follows, secondly, that will and intellect are related to the nature of God as motion and rest, and absolutely as all natural things, which (Prop. 29) must be determined by God to existence and action in a certain manner. For the will, like all other things, needs a cause by which it may be determined to existence and action in a certain manner, and although from a given will or intellect infinite things may follow, God cannot on their account be said to act from freedom of will, any more than God can be said to act from freedom of motion, or rest by reason of the things which follow from motion to rest (for from motion and rest infinite numbers of things follow). Therefore, will does not appertain to the ire of God more than other natural things, but is tied to it as motion and rest and all other things are tied to it; these all following, as we have shown, from necessity of the divine nature, and being determined by existence and action in a certain manner.

PROP. 33. — *Things could have been produced by God in no other manner nor in any other order than that in which they have been produced.*

Schol. 1. — Since I have thus shown, with greater clarity than that of noonday light, that in things there is absolutely nothing by virtue of which they can be called contingent, I wish now to explain in a few words what be understood by *contingent*, but firstly, what is to understood by *necessary* and *impossible*. A thing is *necessary* either in reference to its essence or its cause. Tor the existence of a thing necessarily follows either from the essence and definition of the thing itself, or from a given efficient cause. In the same way a thing is said to be *impossible* either because the essence of the thing itself. or its definition involves a contradiction, or because no external cause exists determinate to the production of such a thing.

But a thing cannot be called *contingent* unless with reference to a deficiency in our knowledge. For if we do not know that the essence of a thing involves a contradiction, or if we actually know that it involves no contradiction, and nevertheless we can affirm nothing with certainty about its existence because the order of causes is concealed from us, that thing can never appear to us either as necessary or impossible, and therefore we call it either contingent or possible.

Schol. 2. — From what has gone before it clearly follows that things have been produced by God in the highest degree of perfection, since they have necessarily followed from the existence of a most perfect nature. Nor does this doctrine accuse God of any imperfection, but. on the contrary, God's perfection has compelled us to affirm it.

PROP. 34. — *The power of God is God's essence itself.*

PROP. 35. — *Whatever we conceive to be in God's power necessarily exists.*

PROP. 36. — *Nothing exists from whose nature an effect does not follow.*

APPENDIX

I have now explained the nature of God and its properties. I have shown that God necessarily exists; that God is one God; that from the necessity alone of God's own nature God is and acts; that God is, and in what way God is, the free cause of all things; that all things are in God, and so depend upon God that without God they can neither be nor can be conceived; and, finally, that all things have been predetermined by God, not indeed from a freedom of will or from absolute good pleasure, but from God's absolute nature or infinite power.

Moreover, wherever an opportunity was afforded, I have endeavoured to remove prejudices which might hinder the perception of the truth of what I have demonstrated; but because not a few still remain which have been and are now sufficient to prove a very great hindrance to the comprehension of the connection of things in the manner in which I have explained it, I have thought it worthwhile to call them up to be examined by reason. But all these prejudices which I here undertake to point out depend upon this solely; that it is commonly supposed that all things in nature, like humans, work to some end; and indeed it is thought to be certain that God directs all things to some sure end, for it is said that God has made all things for human beings, and humans that they may worship God.

This, therefore, I will first investigate by inquiring, firstly, why so many rest in this prejudice, and why all are so naturally inclined to embrace it? I shall then show its falsity, and, finally, the manner in which there have arisen from it prejudices concerning *good* and *evil*, *merit* and *sin, praise* and *blame, order* and *disorder, beauty* and *deformity,* and so forth.

This, however, is not the place to deduce these things from the nature of the human mind. It will be sufficient if I here take as an axiom that which no one ought to dispute, namely, that human beings are born ignorant of the causes of things, and that they have a desire, of which they are conscious, to seek that which is profitable to them. From this it follows, firstly, that they think themselves free because they are conscious of their wishes and appetites, whilst at the same time they are ignorant of the causes by which they are led to wish and desire, not dreaming what they are; and, secondly, it follows that humans do everything for an end, namely, for that which is profitable to them, which is what they seek. Hence it happens that they attempt to discover merely the final causes of that which has happened; and when they have heard them they are satisfied, because there is no longer any cause for further uncertainty. But if they cannot hear from another what these final causes are, nothing remains but to turn to themselves and reflect upon the ends which usually determine them to the like actions, and thus by their own minds they necessarily judge that of another.

Moreover, since they discover, both within and without themselves, a multitude of means which contribute not a little to the attainment of what is profitable to themselves — for example, the eyes, which are useful for seeing, the teeth for mastication, plants and animals for nourishment, the sun for giving light, the sea for feeding fish, &c. — it comes to pass that all natural objects are considered as means for obtaining what is profitable. These too being evidently discovered and not created by humans, hence they have a cause for believing that some other person exists, who has prepared them for human use. For having considered them as means, it was impossible to believe that they had created themselves, and so humans were obliged to infer from the means which they were in the habit of providing for themselves that some ruler or rulers of nature exist, endowed with human liberty, who have taken care of all things for them, and have made all things for their use.

Since they never heard anything about the mind of these rulers, they were compelled to judge of it from their own, and hence they affirmed that the gods direct everything for their advantage, in order that they may be bound to them and hold them in the highest honour. This is the reason why humans have devised for each one of themselves, out of their own brain, a different mode of worshipping God, so that God might love them above others, and direct all nature to the service of their blind cupidity and insatiable avarice.

Thus has this prejudice been turned into a superstition and has driven deep roots into the mind — a prejudice which was the reason why everyone has so eagerly tried to discover and explain the final causes of things. The attempt, however, to show that nature does nothing in vain (that is to say, nothing which is not profitable to humans), seems to end in showing that nature, the gods, and humans are alike mad.

Do but see, I pray, to what all this has led. Amidst so much in nature that is beneficial, not a few things must have been observed which are injurious, such as storms, earthquakes, diseases, and it was affirmed that these things happened either because the gods were angry because of wrongs which had been inflicted on them by humans, or because of sins committed in the method of worshipping them; and although experience daily contradicted this, and showed by an infinity of examples that both the beneficial and the injurious were indiscriminately bestowed on the pious and the impious, the inveterate prejudices on this point have not therefore been abandoned. For it was much easier for humans to place these things aside with others of the use of which they were ignorant, and thus retain their present and inborn state of ignorance, than to destroy the whole superstructure and think out a new one.

Hence it was looked upon as indisputable that the judgments of the gods far surpass our comprehension; and this opinion alone would have been sufficient to keep the human race in darkness to all eternity, if mathematics, which does not deal with ends, but with the essences and properties of forms, had not placed before us another rule of truth. In addition to mathematics, other causes also might be assigned, which it is superfluous here to enumerate, tending to make people reflect upon these universal prejudices, and leading them to a true knowledge of things.

I have thus sufficiently explained what I promised in the first place to explain. There will now be no need of many words to show that nature has set no end before herself and that all final causes are nothing but human actions. For I believe that this is sufficiently evident both from the foundations and causes of this prejudice, and from Prop. 16 and 32, as well as from all those propositions in which I have shown that all things are begotten by a certain eternal necessity of nature and in absolute perfection. Thus much, nevertheless, I will add, that this doctrine concerning an end altogether overturns nature. For that which is in truth the cause it considers as the effect, and *vice versa*.

Again, that which is first in nature it puts last; and, finally, that which is supreme and most perfect it makes the most imperfect. For (passing by the first two assertions as self-evident) it is plain from Props. 21, 22, and 23, that that effect is the most perfect which is immediately produced by God and in proportion as intermediate causes are necessary for the production of a thing is it imperfect but if things which are immediately produced by God were made in order that God might obtain the end God had in view, then the last things for the sake of which the first exist, must be the most perfect of all.

Again, this doctrine does away with God's perfection. For if God works to obtain an end, God necessarily seeks something of which God stands in need. And although theologians and metaphysicians distinguish between the end of want and the end of assimilation (*finem indigentice et finem assimilationis*), they confess that God has done all things for God's own sake, and not for the sake of the things to be created, because before the creation they can assign nothing excepting God for the sake of which God could do anything; and therefore they are necessarily compelled to admit that God stood in need of and desired those things for which God determined to prepare means. This is self-evident.

Nor is it here to be overlooked that the adherents of this doctrine, who have found a pleasure in displaying their ingenuity in assigning the ends of things, have introduced a new species of argument, not the *reductio ad impossible,* but the *reductio ad ignorantiam,* to prove their position, which shows that it had no other method of defense left. For, by way of example, if a stone has fallen from some roof on somebody's head and killed them, they will demonstrate in this manner that the stone has fallen in order to kill the man. For if it did not fall for that purpose by the will of God, how could so many circumstances concur through chance (and a number often simultaneously do concur)?

You will answer, perhaps, that the event happened because the wind blew and the man was passing that way. But, they will urge, why did the wind blow at that time, and why did the man pass that way precisely at the same moment? If you again reply that the wind rose then because the sea on the preceding day began to be stormy, the weather hitherto having been calm, and that the man had been invited by a friend, they will urge again — because there is no end of questioning — But why was the sea agitated? Why was the man invited at that time? And so they will not cease from asking the causes of causes, until at last you fly to the will of God, the refuge for ignorance.

So, also, when they behold the structure of the human body they are amazed; and because they are ignorant of the causes of such art, they conclude that the body was made not by mechanical but by a supernatural or divine art, and has been formed in such a way so that the one part may not injure the other. Hence it happens that the person who endeavours to find out the true causes of miracles, and who desires as a wise person to understand nature, and not to gape at it like a fool, is generally considered and proclaimed to be a heretic and impious by those whom the vulgar worship as the interpreters both of nature and the gods. For these know that if ignorance be removed, amazed stupidity, the sole ground on which they rely in arguing or in defending their authority, is taken away also. But these things I leave and pass on to that which I determined to do in the third place.

After humans have persuaded themselves that all things which exist are made for them, they must in everything adjudge that to be of the greatest importance which is most useful to them, and they must esteem that to be of surpassing worth by which they are most beneficially affected. In this way they are compelled to form those notions by which they explain nature; such, for instance, as *good, evil, order, confusion, heat, cold, beauty, and deformity, &c.;* and because they suppose themselves to be free, notions like those of *praise and blame, sin and merit,* have arisen. These latter I shall hereafter explain when I have treated of human nature; the former I will here briefly unfold.

It is to be observed that humans have given the name *good* to everything which leads to health and the worship of God; on the contrary, everything which does not lead thereto they call *evil*. But because those who do not understand nature affirm nothing about things themselves, but only imagine them, and take the imagination to be understanding, they therefore, ignorant of things and their nature, firmly believe an *order* to be in things; for when things are so placed that, if they are represented to us through the senses, we can easily imaging them, and consequently easily remember them, we call them well arranged; but if they are not placed so that we can imagine and remember them, we call them badly arranged or *confused.*

Moreover, since those things are more especially pleasing to us which we can easily imagine, people therefore prefer order to confusion, as if order were something in nature apart from our own imagination; and they say that God has created everything in order, and in this manner they ignorantly attribute imagination to God, unless they mean perhaps that God, out of consideration for the human imagination, has disposed things in the manner in which they can most easily be imagined. No hesitation either seems to be caused by the fact that an infinite number of things are discovered which far surpass our imagination, and very many which confound it through its weakness. But enough of this.

The other notions which I have mentioned are nothing but modes in which the imagination is affected in different ways, and nevertheless they are regarded by the ignorant as being specially attributes of things, because, as we have remarked, humans consider all things as made for themselves, and call the nature of a thing good, evil, sound, putrid, or corrupt, just as they are affected by it. For example, if the motion by which the nerves are affected by means of objects represented to the eye conduces to well-being, the objects by which it is caused are called *beautiful;* while those exciting a contrary motion are called *deformed*. Those things, too, which stimulate the senses through the nostrils are called sweet-smelling or stinking; those which act through the taste are called sweet or bitter, full-flavoured or insipid; those which act through the touch, hard or soft, heavy or light; those, lastly, which act through the ears are said to make a noise, sound, or harmony, the last having caused humans to lose their senses to such a degree that they have believed that God even is delighted with it. Indeed, philosophers may be found who have persuaded themselves that the celestial motions beget a harmony. All these things sufficiently show that everyone judges things by the constitution of their brain, or rather accepts the affections of their imagination in the place of things.

It is not, therefore, to be wondered at, as we may observe in passing, that all those controversies which we see have arisen amongst people, so that at last skepticism has been the result. For although human bodies agree in many things, they differ in more, and therefore that which to one person is good will appear to another evil, that which to one is well arranged to another is confused, that which pleases one will displease another, and so on in other cases which I pass by both because we cannot notice them at length here, and because they are within the experience of everyone. For everyone has heard the expressions: So many heads, so many ways of thinking; Everyone is satisfied with their own way of thinking; Differences of brains are not less common than differences of taste — all which show that people decide upon matters according to the constitution of their brains, and imagine rather than understand things. If humans understood things, they would, as mathematics proves, at least be all alike convinced if they were not all alike attracted.

We see, therefore, that all those methods by which the common people are in the habit of explaining nature are only different sorts of imaginations, and do not reveal the nature of anything in itself, but only the constitution of the imagination; and because they have names as if they were entities existing apart from the imagination, I call them entities not of the reason but of the imagination. All argument, therefore, urged against us based upon such notions can be easily refuted. Many people, for instance, are accustomed to argue thus; — If all things have followed from the necessity of the most perfect nature of God, how is it that so many imperfections have arisen in nature — corruption, for instance, of things till they stink; deformity, exciting disgust; confusion, evil, crime, &c.?

But, as I have just observed, all this is easily answered. For the perfection of things is to be judged by their nature and power alone; nor are they more or less perfect because they delight or offend the human senses, or because they are beneficial or prejudicial to human nature. But to those who ask why God has not created all people in such a manner that they might be controlled by the dictates of reason alone, I give but this answer: because to God material was not wanting for the creation of everything, from the highest down to the very lowest grade of perfection; or, to speak more properly, because the laws of God's nature were so ample that they sufficed for the production of everything which can be conceived by an infinite intellect, as I have demonstrated in Prop. 16.

These are the prejudices which I undertook to notice here. If any others of a similar character remain, they can easily be rectified with a little thought by any one.

END OF THE FIRST PART

ETHICS
AN OUTLINE

Second Part

OF THE NATURE AND ORIGIN OF THE MIND

OF THE NATURE AND ORIGIN OF THE MIND

I PASS on now to explain those things which must necessarily follow from the essence of God or the Being eternal and infinite; not indeed to explain all these things, for we have demonstrated (Prop. 16, pt. 1) that an infinitude of things must follow in an infinite number of ways, — but to consider those things only which may conduct us as it were by the hand to a knowledge of the human mind and its highest happiness.

DEFINITIONS

I. By **body,** I understand a mode which expresses in a certain and determinate manner the essence of God in so far as it is considered as the thing extended. (See Corol. Prop. 25, pt. 1)

II. I say that to the **essence** of anything pertains that, which being given, the thing itself is necessarily posited, and being taken away, the thing is necessarily taken; or, in other words, that, without which the thing can neither be nor be conceived, and which in its turn cannot be nor be conceived without the thing.

III. By **idea,** I understand a conception of the mind which the mind forms because it is a thinking thing.

Explanation. — I use the word, conception rather than perception because the name perception seems to indicate that the mind is passive in its relation to the object. But the word conception seems to express the action of the mind.

IV. By **adequate idea**, I understand an idea which, in so far as it is considered in itself, without reference to the object, has all the properties or internal signs (*denominationes intrinsecas*) of a true idea.

Explanation. — I say internal, so as to exclude that which is external, the agreement, namely, of the idea with its object.

V. **Duration** is the indefinite continuation of existence.

Explanation. — I call it indefinite because it cannot be determined by the nature itself of the existing thing nor by the efficient cause, which necessarily posits the existence of the thing but does not take it away.

VI. By **reality and perfection** I understand the same thing.

VII. By **individual things** I understand things which are finite and which have a determinate existence; and if a number of individuals so unite in one action that they are all simultaneously the cause of one effect, I consider them all, so far, as a one individual thing.

AXIOMS

I. The essence of human beings does not involve necessary existence; that is to say, the existence as well as the non-existence of this or that person may or may not follow from the order of nature.

II. Human beings think.

III. Modes of thought, such as love, desire, or the affections of the mind, by whatever name they may be called, do not exist, unless in the same individual the idea exist of a thing loved, desired, &c. But the idea may exist although no other mode of thinking exist

IV. We perceive that a certain body is affected in many ways.

V. No individual things are felt or perceived by us excepting bodies and modes of thought.

The postulates will be found after Proposition 13.

THE NATURE AND ORIGIN OF THE MIND

PROP. 1. — *Thought is an attribute of God, or God is a thinking thing.*

Schol. — This proposition is plain from the fact that we can conceive an infinite thinking Being. For the more things a thinking being can think, the more reality or perfection we conceive it to possess, and therefore the being which can think an infinitude of things in infinite ways is necessarily infinite by their power of thinking.

PROP. 2. — *Extension is an attribute of God, or God is an extended thing.*

PROP. 3. — *In God there necessarily exists the idea of God's essence, and of all things which necessarily follow from God's essence.*

Schol. — The common people understand by God's power God's free will and right over all existing things, which are therefore commonly looked upon as contingent; for they say that God has the power of destroying everything and reducing it to nothing. They very frequently, too, compare God's power with the power of kings. [...] However, we have shown that God does everything with that necessity with which God understands Godself; that is to say, as it follows from the necessity of the divine nature that God understands Godself (a truth admitted by all), so by the same necessity it follows that God does an infinitude of things in infinite ways. Moreover, in Prop. 34, we have shown that the power of God is nothing but the active essence of God, and therefore it is as impossible for us to conceive that God does not act as that God does not exist If it pleased me to go farther, I could show besides that the power which the common people ascribe to God is not only a human power (which shows that they look upon God as a man, or as being like a man), but that it also involves weakness.

PROP. 4. — *The idea of God from which infinite members of things follow in infinite ways, can be one only.*

PROP. 5. — *The formal Being of ideas recognises God for its cause in so far only as God is considered as a thinking thing, and not in so far as God is explained by any other attribute; that is to say, the ideas both of God's attributes and of individual things do not recognise as their efficient cause the objects of the ideas or the things which are perceived, but God Godself in so far as God is a thinking thing.*

PROP. 6. — *The modes of any attribute have God for a cause only in so far as God is considered under that attribute of which they are modes, and not in so far as God is considered under any other attribute.*

PROP. 7. — *The order and connection of ideas is the same as the order and connection of things.*

Corol. — Hence it follows that God's power of thinking is equal to God's actual power of acting; that is to say, whatever follows *formally* from the infinite nature of God, follows from the idea of God [*idea Dei*], in the same order and in the same connection *objectively* in God.

PROP. 8. — *The ideas of non-existent individual things or modes are comprehended in the infinite idea of God in the same way that the formal essences of individual things or modes are contained in the attributes of God.*

PROP. 9. — *The idea of an individual thing actually existing has God for a cause, not in so far as God is infinite, but in so far as God is considered to be affected by another idea of an individual thing actually existing, of which idea also God is the cause in so far as God is affected by a thirds and so on* ad infinitum.

PROP. 10. — *The Being of substance does not pertain to the essence of a human being or, in other words, substance does not constitute the form of a human being.*

Corol. — Hence it follows that the essence of human beings consists of certain modifications of the attributes of God; for the Being of substance does not pertain to the essence of humans. It is therefore something which is in God, and which without God can neither be nor be conceived, or an affection or mode which expresses the nature of God in a certain and determinate manner.

Schol.— Everyone must admit that without God nothing can be nor be conceived; for everyone admits that God is the sole cause both of the essence and of the existence of all things; that is to say, God is not only the cause of things, to use a common expression, *secundum fieri,* but also *secundum esse.*

PROP. 11. — *The first thing which forms the actual Being of the human mind is nothing else than the idea of an individual thing actually existing.*

Corol.— Hence it follows that the human mind is a part of the infinite intellect of God, and therefore, when we say that the human mind perceives this or that thing, we say nothing else than that God has this or that idea; not indeed in so far as God is infinite, but in so far as God is explained through the nature of the human mind, or in so far as God forms the essence of the human mind; and when we say that God has this or that idea, not merely in so far as God forms the nature of the human mind, but in so far as God has at the same time with the human mind the idea also of another thing, then we say that the human mind perceives the thing partially or inadequately.

PROP. 12. — *Whatever happens in the object of the idea constituting the human mind must be perceived by the human mind; or, in other words, an idea of that thing will necessarily existin the human mind. That is to say, if the object of the idea constituting the human mind be a body, nothing can happen in that body which is not perceived by the mind.*

PROP. 13. — *The object of the idea constituting the human mind is a body, or a certain mode of extension actually existing, and nothing else.*

Corol. — Hence it follows that human beings are composed of mind and body, and that the human body exists as we perceive it.

Schol. — Hence we see not only that the human mind is united to the body, but also what is to be understood by the union of the mind and body. But no one can understand it adequately or distinctly without knowing adequately beforehand the nature of our body; for those things which we have proved hitherto are altogether general, nor do they refer more to human beings than to other individuals, all of which are animate, although in different degrees. For of everything there necessarily exists in God an idea of which God is the cause, in the same way as the idea of the human body exists in God and therefore everything that we have said of the idea of the human body is. necessarily true of the idea of any other thing.

We cannot, however, deny that ideas, like objects themselves, differ from one another, and that one is more excellent and contains more reality than another, just as the object of one idea is more excellent and contains more reality than another. Therefore, in order to determine the difference between the human mind and other things and its superiority over them, we must first know, as we have said, the nature of its object, that is to say, the nature of the human body. I am not able to explain it here, nor is such an explanation necessary for what I wish to demonstrate. Thus much, nevertheless, I will say generally, that in proportion as one body is better adapted than another to do or suffer many things, in the same proportion will the mind at the same time be better adapted to perceive many things, and the more the actions of a body depend upon itself alone, and the less other bodies co-operate with it in action, the better adapted will the mind be for distinctly understanding.

We can thus determine the superiority of one mind to another; we can also see the why we have only a very confused knowledge of our body, together with many other things which I shall deduce in what follows. For this reason I have thought it worthwhile more accurately to explain and demonstrate the truths just mentioned, to which end it is necessary for me to say beforehand a few words upon the nature of bodies.

AXIOM 1. — All bodies are either in a state of motion or rest.

AXIOM 2.—Every body moves, sometimes slowly, sometimes quickly.

LEMMA I. — *Bodies are distinguished from one another in respect of motion and rest, quickness and slowness, and not in respect of substance.*

LEMMA II. — *All bodies agree in some respects.*

LEMMA III. — *A body in motion or at rest must be determined to motion or rest by another body, which was also determined to motion or rest by another, and that in its turn by another, and so on* ad infinitum.

AXIOM 1. — All the modes by which one body is affected by another follow from the nature of the body affected, and at the same time from the nature of the affecting body, so that one and the same body may be moved in different ways according to the diversity of the nature of the moving bodies, and, on the other hand, so that different bodies may be moved in different ways by one and the same body.

AXIOM 2. — When a body in motion strikes against another which is at rest and immovable, it is reflected, in order that it may continue its motion, and the angle of the line of reflected motion with the plane of the body at rest against which it struck will be equal to the angle which the line of the motion of incidence makes with the same plane.

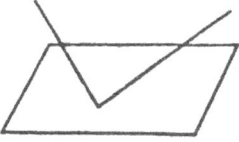

Thus much for simplest bodies which are distinguished from one another by motion and rest, speed and slowness alone; let us now advance to composite bodies.

DEFINITION. — When a number of bodies of the same or of different magnitudes are pressed together by others, so that they lie one upon the other, or if they are in motion with the same or with different degrees of speed, so that they communicate their motion to one another in a certain fixed proportion, these bodies are said to be mutually united, and taken altogether they are said to compose one body or individual, which is distinguished from other bodies by this union of bodies.

AXIOM 3. — Whether it is easy or difficult to force the parts composing an individual to change their situation, and consequently whether it is easy or difficult for the individual to change its shape, depends upon whether the parts of the individual or of the compound body lie with less, or whether they lie with greater surfaces upon one another. Hence bodies whose parts lie upon each other with greater surfaces I will call *hard*; those *soft,* whose parts lie on one another with smaller surfaces; and those *fluid,* whose parts move amongst each other.

LEMMA. IV. — *If a certain number of bodies be separated from the body or individual which is composed of a number of bodies, and if their place be supplied by the same number of other bodies of the same nature, the individual will retain the nature which it had before without any change of form.*

LEMMA. V. — *If the parts composing an individual become greater or less proportionately, so that they preserve towards one another the same kind of motion and rest, the individual will also retain the nature which it had before without any change of form.*

LEMMA. VI. — *If any number of bodies composing an individual are compelled to divert into one direction the motion they previously had in another, but are nevertheless able to continue and reciprocally communicate their motions in the same manner as before, the individual will then retain its nature without any change of form.*

LEMMA. VII. — *The individual thus composed will, moreover, retain its nature whether it more as a whole or be at rest, or whether it mow in this or that direction, provided that each part retain its own motion and communicate it as before to the rest.*

Postulate 1. — The human body is composed of a number of individuals of diverse nature, each of which is composite to a high degree.

Postulate 2. — Of the individuals of which the human body is composed, some are fluid, some soft, and some hard.

Postulate 3. — The individuals composing the human body, and consequently the human body itself, are affected by external bodies in many ways.

Postulate 4. — The human body needs for its preservation many other bodies by which it is, as it were, continually regenerated.

Postulate 5. — When a fluid part of the human body is determined by an external body, so that it often strikes upon another which is soft, the fluid part changes the plane of the soft part, and leaves upon it, as it were, some traces of the impelling external body.

Postulate 6. — The human body can move and arrange external bodies in many ways.

PROP. 14. — *The human mind is adapted to the perception of many things, and its aptitude increases in proportion to the number of ways in which its body can be disposed.*

Corol. 1. — Hence it follows, in the first place, that the human mind perceives the nature of many bodies together with that of its own body.

Corol. 2. — It follows, secondly, that the ideas we have of external bodies indicate the constitution of our own body rather than the nature of external bodies.

PROP. 15. — *The idea which constitutes the formal Being of the human mind is not simple, but is composed of a number of ideas.*

Corol. — The mind is able to contemplate external things by which the human body was once affected as if they were present, although they are not present and do not exist.

PROP. 16. — *The idea of every way in which the human body is affected by external bodies must involve the nature of the human body, and at the same time the nature of the external body.*

PROP. 17. — *If the human body be affected in a way which involves the nature of any external body, the human mind will contemplate that external body as actually existing or as present, until the human body be affected by an affect which excludes the existence or presence of the external body.*

PROP. 18. — *If the human body has at any time been simultaneously affected by two or more bodies, whenever the mind afterwards imagines one of them, it will also remember the others.*

Schol. — We clearly understand by this what *memory* is. It is nothing else than a certain concatenation of ideas, involving the nature of things which are outside the human body, a concatenation which corresponds in the mind to the order and concatenation of the affections of the human body. I say, firstly, that it is a concatenation of those ideas only which involve the nature of things which are outside the human body, and not of those ideas which explain the nature of those things, for there are in truth (Prop. 16) ideas of the affections of the human body, which involve its nature as well as the nature of external bodies.

I say, in the second place, that this concatenation takes place according to the order and concatenation of the affections of the human body, that I may distinguish it from the concatenation of ideas which takes place according to the order of the intellect, and enables the mind to perceive things through their first causes, and is the same in all people. Hence we can clearly understand how it is that the mind from the thought of one thing at once turns to the thought of another within which is not in any way like the first.

For example, from the thought of the word *pomum* a Roman immediately turned to the thought of the fruit, which has no resemblance to the articulate sound *pomum* nor anything in common with it, excepting this, that the body of that man was often affected by the thing and the sound; that is to say, he often heard the word *pomum* when he saw the fruit. In this manner each person will turn from one thought to another according to the manner in which the habit of each has arranged the images of things in the body.

The soldier, for instance, if he sees the footsteps of a horse in the sand, will immediately turn from the thought of a horse to the thought of a horseman, and so to the thought of war. The countryman, on the other hand, from the thought of a horse will turn to the thought of their plough, their field, &c.; and thus each person will turn from one thought to this or that thought, according to the manner in which they have been accustomed to connect and bind together the images of things in their mind.

PROP. 19. — *The human mind does not know the human body itself, nor does it know that the body exists except. through ideas of affections by which the body is affected.*

PROP. 20. — *There exists in God the idea or knowledge of the human mind, which follows in God, and is related to God in the same way as the idea or knowledge of the human body.*

PROP. 21. — *This idea of the mind is united to the mind in the same way as the mind itself is united to the body.*

We have there shown that the idea of the body and the body, that is to say (Prop. 13), the mind and the body, are one and the same individual, which at one time is considered under the attribute of thought, and at another under that of extension; the idea of the mind, therefore, and the mind itself are one and the same thing, which is considered under one and the same attribute, that of thought. It follows, I say, that the idea of the mind and the mind itself exist in God from the same necessity and from the same power of thought. For, indeed, the idea of the mind, that is to say, the idea of the idea, is nothing but the form of the idea in so far as this is considered as a mode of thought and without relation to the object; just as persons who know anything, by that very fact know that they know, and know that they know that they know, and so on *ad infinitum.*

PROP. 22. — *The human mind not only perceives the affections of the body, but also the ideas of these affections.*

PROP. 23. — *The mind does not know itself except in so far as it perceives the ideas of the affections of the body.*

PROP. 24. — *The human mind does not involve an adequate knowledge of the parts composing the human body.*

PROP. 25. — *The idea of each affection of the human body does not involve an adequate knowledge of an external body.*

PROP. 26. — *The human mind perceives no external body as actually existing, unless through the ideas of the affections of its body.*

PROP. 27. — *The idea of any affection of the human body does not involve an adequate knowledge of the human body itself.*

PROP. 28. — *The ideas of the affections of the human body, in so far as they are related only to the human mind are not dear and distinct, but confused.*

PROP. 29. — *The idea of the idea of any affection of the human body does not involve an adequate knowledge of the human mind.*

Corol. — From this it is evident that the human mind, when it perceives things in the common order of nature, has no adequate knowledge of itself nor of its own body, nor of external bodies, but only a confused and mutilated knowledge; for the mind does not know itself unless in so far as it perceives the ideas of the affections of the body . Moreover (Prop. 19), it does not perceive its body unless through those same ideas of the affections by means of which alone (Prop. 26) it perceives external bodies. Therefore in so far as it possesses these ideas it possesses an adequate knowledge neither of itself (Prop. 29), nor of its body (Prop. 27), nor of external bodies (Prop. 25), but merely (Prop. 28 a mutilated and confused knowledge.

Schol.— I say expressly that the mind has no adequate knowledge of itself, nor of its body, nor of external bodies, but only a confused knowledge, as often as it perceives things in the common order of nature, that is to say, as often as it is determined to the contemplation of this or that *externally* — namely, by a chance coincidence, and not as often as it is determined *internally* — for the reason that it contemplates several things at once, and is determined to understand in what they differ, agree, or oppose one another; for whenever it is internally disposed in this or in any other way, it then contemplates things clearly and distinctly, as I shall show presently.

PROP. 30. — *About the duration of our body we can have but a very inadequate knowledge.*

PROP. 31. — *About the duration of individual things which are outside us we can have but a very inadequate knowledge.*

Corol. — Hence it follows that all individual things are contingent and corruptible, for we can have no adequate knowledge concerning their duration (Prop. 31), and this is what is to be understood by us as their contingency and capability of corruption; for (Prop. 29) there is no other contingency but this.

PROP. 32. — *All ideas, in so far as they are related to God, are true.*

PROP. 33. — *In ideas there is nothing positive on account of which they are called false.*

PROP. 34. — *Every idea which in us is absolute, that is to say, adequate and perfect, is true.*

PROP. 35. — *Falsity consists in the privation of knowledge, which inadequate, that is to say, mutilated and confused ideas involve.*

For instance, people are deceived because they think themselves free, and the sole reason for thinking so is that they are conscious of their own actions, and ignorant of the causes by which those actions are determined. Their idea of liberty therefore is this — that they know no cause for their own actions; for as to saying that their actions depend upon their will, these are words to which no idea is attached. What the will is, and in what manner it moves the body, everyone is ignorant, for those who pretend otherwise, and devise seats and dwelling-places of the soul, usually excite our laughter or disgust.

Just in the same manner, when we look at the sun, we imagine their distance from us to be about 200 feet; the error not consisting solely in the imagination, but arising from our not knowing what the true distance is when we imagine, and what are the causes of our imagination. For although we may afterwards know that the sun is more than 600 diameters of the earth distant from us, we still imagine it near us, since we imagine it to be so near, not because we are ignorant of its true distance, but because an affection of our body involves the essence of the sun, in so far as our body itself is affected by it.

PROP. 36. — *Inadequate and confused ideas follow by the same necessity as adequate or dear and distinct ideas.*

PROP. 37. —*That which is common to everything {see Lemma 2), and which is equally in the part and in the whole, forms the essence of no individual thing.*

PROP. 38. — *Those things which are common to everything, and which are equally in the part and in the whole, can only be adequately conceived.*

PROP. 39. — *There will exist in the human mind an adequate idea of that which is common and proper to the human body, and to any external bodies by which the human body is generally affected — of that which equally in the part of each of these external bodies and in the whole is common and proper.*

Corol. — Hence it follows that the more things the body has in common with other bodies, the more things will the mind be adapted to perceive.

PROP. 40. — *Those ideas are also adequate which follow in the mind from ideas which are adequate in it.*

Schol. — I have thus explained the origin of those notions which are called *common,* and which are the foundations of our reasoning; but of some axioms or notions other causes exist which it would be advantageous to explain by our method, for we should thus be able to distinguish those notions which are more useful than others, and those which are scarcely of any use; those which are common;

those which are clear and distinct only to those persons who do not suffer from prejudice; and, finally, those which are ill-founded.

Moreover, it would be manifest whence these notions which are called *second,* and consequently the axioms founded upon them, have taken their origin, and other things, too, would be explained which I have thought about these matters at different times. Since, however, I have set apart this subject for another treatise, and because I do not wish to create disgust with excessive prolixity, I have determined to pass by this matter here.

But not to omit anything which is necessary for us to know, I will briefly give the causes from which terms called *Transcendental,* such as *Being, Thing, Something,* have taken their origin. These terms have arisen because the human body, inasmuch as it is limited, can form distinctly in itself a certain number only of images at once. If this number be exceeded, the images will become confused; and if the number of images which the body is able to form distinctly be greatly exceeded, they will all run one into another. Since this is so, it is clear that in proportion to the number of images which can be formed at the same time in the body will be the number of bodies which the human mind can imagine at the same time.

If the images in the body, therefore, are all confused, the mind will confusedly imagine all the bodies without distinguishing the one from the other, and will include them all, as it were, under one attribute, that of being or thing. The same confusion may also be caused by lack of uniform force in the images and from other analogous causes, which there is no need to discuss here, the consideration of one cause being sufficient for the purpose we have in view. For it all comes to this, that these terms signify ideas in the highest degree confused.

It is in this way that those notions have arisen which are called *Universal* such as, *Man, Horse, Dog,* &c.; that is to say, so many images of people, for instance, are formed in the human body at once, that they exceed the power of the imagination, not entirely, but to such a degree that the mind has no power to imagine the determinate number of people and the small differences of each, such as colour and size, &c. It will therefore distinctly imagine that only in which all of them agree in so far as the body is affected by them, for by that the body was chiefly affected, that is to say, by each individual, and this it will express by the name man, covering thereby an infinite number of individuals; to imagine a determinate number of individuals being out of its power.

But we must observe that these notions are not formed by all persons in the same way, but that they vary in each case according to the thing by which the body is more frequently affected, and which the mind more easily imagines or recollects. For example, those who have more frequently looked with admiration upon the stature of humans, by the name human will understand an animal of erect stature, while those who have been in the habit of fixing their thoughts on something else, will form another common image of humans, describing a human being, for instance, as an animal capable of laughter, a biped without feathers, a rational animal, and so on; each person forming universal images of things according to the temperament of their own body. It is not therefore to be wondered at that so many controversies have arisen amongst those philosophers who have endeavoured to explain natural objects by the images of things alone.

Schol. 2. — 'From what has been already said, it clearly appears that we perceive many things and form universal ideas:

1. From individual things, represented by the senses to us in a mutilated and confused manner, and without order to the intellect. These perceptions I have therefore been in the habit of calling *knowledge from vague experience.*

2. From signs; as, for example, when we hear or read certain words, we recollect things and form certain ideas of them similar to them, through which ideas we imagine things. These two ways of looking at things I shall hereafter call *knowledge of the first kind, opinion or imagination.*

3. From our possessing common notions and adequate ideas of the properties of things. This I shall call reason and *knowledge of the second kind.*

Besides these two kinds of knowledge, there is a *third,* as I shall hereafter show, which we shall call *intuitive science.* This kind of knowing advances from an adequate idea of the formal essence of certain attributes of God to the adequate knowledge of the essence of things.

PROP. 41. — *Knowledge of the first kind alone is the cause of falsity; knowledge of the second and third orders is necessarily true,*

PROP. 42. — *it is the knowledge of the second and third, and not that of the first kind, which teaches this to distinguish the true from the false.*

PROP. 43. — *Human beings who have a true idea knows at the same time that they have a true idea, nor can they doubt the truth of the thing.*

Schol. [...] No one who has a true idea is ignorant that a true idea involves the highest certitude; to have a true idea signifying just this, to know a thing perfectly as well as possible. No one, in fact, can doubt this, unless they suppose an idea to be something dumb, like a picture on a tablet, instead of being a mode of thought, that is to say, intelligence itself. Moreover, I ask who can know that they understand a thing unless they first of all understand that thing? That is to say, who can know that they are certain of anything unless they are first of all certain of that thing?

Then, again, what true idea can be given more clearly and surely which shall be the standard of truth? Just as light reveals both itself and the darkness, so truth is the standard of itself and of the false. I consider what has been said to be a sufficient answer to the objection that if a true idea is distinguished from a false idea only in so far as it is said to agree with that of which it is the idea, the true idea therefore has no reality nor perfection above the false idea (since they are distinguished by an external sign alone), and consequently the person who has true ideas will have no greater reality or perfection than another person who has false ideas only.

We must remember, besides, that our mind, in so far as it truly perceives things, is a part of the infinite intellect of God, and therefore it must be that the clear and distinct ideas of the mind are as true as those of God.

PROP. 44. — *It is not of the nature of reason to consider things as contingent but as necessary.*

Corol. 1 — Hence it follows that it is through the imagination alone that we look upon things as *contingent* both with reference to the past and the future.

Corol. 2. — It is of the nature of reason to perceive things under a certain form of *eternity.*

PROP. 45. — *Every idea of any body or actually existing individual thing necessarily involves the eternal and infinite essence of God.*

PROP. 46. — *The knowledge of the eternal and infinite essence of God which each idea involves is adequate and perfect.*

PROP. 47. — *The human mind possesses an adequate knowledge of the eternal and infinite essence of God.*

Schol. — Hence we see that the infinite essence and the eternity of God are known to all; and since all things are in God and are conceived through God, it follows that we can deduce from this knowledge many things which we can know adequately, and that we can thus form that third sort of knowledge of whose excellence and value the Fifth Part will be the place to speak. The reason why we do not possess a knowledge of God as distinct as that which we have of common notions is, that we cannot imagine God as we can bodies; and because we have attached the name God to the images of things which we are in the habit of seeing, an error we can hardly avoid, inasmuch as we are continually affected by external bodies.

Many errors, of a truth, consist merely in the application of the wrong names to things. For if a person says that the lines which are drawn from the centre of the circle to the circumference are not equal, they understand by the circle at all events for the time, something else than mathematicians understand by it. So when humans make errors in calculation, the numbers which are in their minds are not those which are upon the paper. As far as their mind is concerned there is no error, although it seems as if there were, because we think that the numbers in their minds are those which are upon the paper. If we did not think so, we should not believe them to be in error.

For example, when I lately heard a man complaining that their court had flown into one of their neighbour's fowls, I understood what he meant, and therefore did not imagine him be in error. This is the source from which so many controversies arise — that people either do not properly explain their own thoughts, or do not properly interpret those of other people; for, in truth, when they most contradict one another, they either think the same things or something different, so that those things which they suppose to be errors and absurdities in another person are not so.

PROP. 48. — *In the mind there is no absolute or free will, but the mind is determined to this or that volition by a cause, which is also determined by another cause, and this again by another, and so on* ad infinitum.

Schol. — In the same manner it is demonstrated that in the mind there exists no absolute faculty of understanding, desiring, loving, &c. These and the like faculties therefore, are either altogether fictitious, or else are nothing but metaphysical or universal entities, which we are in the habit of forming from individual cases. The intellect and will, therefore, are related to this or that idea or volition as rockiness is related to this or that rock, or as human is related to Peter or Paul. The reason why people imagine themselves to be free we have explained in the Appendix to the First Part. Before, however, I advance any farther, I must observe that by the will I understand a faculty of affirming or denying, but not a desire; a faculty, I say, by which the mind affirms or denies that which is true or false, and not a desire by which the mind seeks a thing or turns away from it.

PROP. 49. — *In the mind there is no volition or affirmation and negation excepting that which the idea, in so far as it is an idea, involves.*

Corol. — The will and the intellect are one and the same.

Schol. — I have thus removed what is commonly thought to be the cause of error. It has been proved above that falsity consists solely in the privation which mutilated and confused ideas involve. A false idea, therefore, in so far as it is false, does not involve certitude. Consequently, when we say that a person assents to what is false and does not doubt it, we do not say that they are certain, but merely that they do not doubt, that is to say, that they assent to what is false, because there are no causes sufficient to make their imagination waver. Although, therefore, a person may be supposed to adhere to what is false, we shall never on that account say that they are certain. For by certitude we understand something positive and not the privation of doubt; but by the privation of certitude we understand falsity.

I warn my readers carefully to distinguish between an idea or conception of the mind and the images of things formed by our imagination. [...] It is necessary that we should distinguish between ideas and the words by which things are signified. For it is because these three things, images, words, and ideas, are by many people either altogether confounded or not distinguished with sufficient accuracy and care that such ignorance exists about this doctrine of the will, so necessary to be known both for the purposes of speculation and for the wise government of life. Those who think that ideas consist of images, which are formed in us by meeting with external bodies, persuade themselves that those ideas of things of which we can form no similar image are not ideas, but mere fancies constructed by the free power of the will.

They look upon ideas, therefore, as dumb pictures on a tablet, and being prepossessed with this prejudice, they do not see that an idea, in so far as it is an idea, involves affirmation or negation. Again, those who confound words with the idea, or with the affirmation itself which the idea involves, think that they can will contrary to their perception, because they affirm or deny something in words alone contrary to their perception. It will be easy for us, however, to divest ourselves of these prejudices if we attend to the nature of thought, which in no way involves the conception of extension, and by doing this we'd clearly see that an idea, since it is a mode of thought, is not an image of anything, nor does it consist of words. For the essence of words and images is formed of bodily motions alone, which involve in no way whatever the conception of thought.

It remains for me now to show what service to our own lives knowledge of this doctrine is. This we shall easily understand from the remarks which follow.

Notice —

1. It is of service in so far as it teaches us that we do everything by the will of God alone, and that we are partakers of the divine nature in proportion as our actions become more and more perfect and we more and more understand God. This doctrine, therefore, besides giving repose in every way to the soul, has also this advantage, that it teaches us in what our highest happiness or blessedness consists, namely, in the knowledge of God alone, by which we are drawn to do those things only which love and piety persuade. Hence we clearly see how greatly those stray from the true estimation of virtue who expect to be distinguished by God with the highest rewards for virtue and the noblest actions as if for the completest servitude, just as if virtue itself and the service of God were not happiness itself and the highest liberty.

2. It is of service to us in so far as it teaches us how we ought to behave with regard to the things of fortune, or those which are not in our power, that is to say, which do not follow from our own nature; for it teaches us with equal mind to wait for and bear each form of fortune, because we know that all things follow from the eternal decree of God, according to that same necessity by which it follows from the essence of a triangle that its three angles are equal to two right angles.

3. This doctrine contributes to the welfare of our social existence, since it teaches us to hate no one, to despise no one, to mock no one, to be angry with no one, and to envy no one. It teaches everyone, moreover, to be content with their own, and to be helpful to their neighbour, not from any womanish pity, from partiality, or superstition, but by the guidance of reason alone, according to the demand of time and circumstance, as I shall show in the Third Part.

4. This doctrine contributes not a little to the advantage of common society, in so far as it teaches us by what means citizens are to be governed and led; not in order that they may be slaves, but that they may freely do those things which are best.

Thus I have discharged the obligation laid upon me in this scholium, and with it I make an end of the Second Part, in which I think that I have explained the nature of the human mind and its properties at sufficient length, and, considering the difficulties of the subject, with sufficient clearness. I think, too, that certain truths have been established, from which much that is noble, most useful, and necessary to be known can be deduced, as we shall partly see from what follows.

END OF THE SECOND PART

ETHICS
AN OUTLINE

Third Part

ON THE ORIGIN AND NATURE OF THE AFFECTS

ON THE ORIGIN AND NATURE OF THE AFFECTS

Most persons who have written about the affects and human conduct of life seem to discuss, not the natural things which follow the common laws of nature, but things which are outside her. They seem indeed to consider human beings in nature as a kingdom within a kingdom. For they believe that humans disturb rather than follow her order; that they have an absolute power over their own actions; and that they are altogether self-determined. They then proceed to attribute the cause of human weakness and changeableness, not to the common power of nature, but to some vice of human nature, which they therefore bewail, laugh at, mock, or, as is more generally the case, detest; whilst they who know how to revile most eloquently or subtly the wellness of the mind are looked upon as divine.

It is true that very eminent persons have not been wanting, to whose labour and industry we confess ourselves much indebted, who have written many excellent things about the right conduct of life, and who have given to mortals counsels full of prudence, but no one so far as I know has determined the nature and strength of the affects, and what the mind is able to do towards controlling them. I remember, indeed, that the celebrated Descartes, although he believed that the mind is absolute master over its own actions, tried nevertheless to explain by their first causes human affects, and at the same time to show the way by which the mind could obtain absolute power over them; but in my opinion they have shown nothing but the acuteness of their great intellect, as I shall make evident in the proper place, for I wish to return to those who prefer to detest and scoff at human affects and actions than understand them. To such as these it will doubtless seem a marvelous thing for me to endeavour to treat by a geometrical method the vices and follies of people, and to desire by a sure method to demonstrate those things which these people cry out against as being opposed to reason, or as being vanities, absurdities, and monstrosities. The following is my reason for so doing.

Nothing happens in nature which can be attributed to any vice of nature, for they are always the same and everywhere one. Her virtue is the same, and her power of acting; that is to say, her laws and rules, according to which all things are and are changed from form to form, are everywhere and always the same; so that there must also be one and the same method of understanding the nature of all things whatsoever, that is to say, by the universal laws and rules of nature. The affects, therefore, of hatred, anger, envy, considered in themselves, follow from the same necessity and virtue of nature as other individual things; they have therefore certain causes through which they are to be understood, and certain properties which are just as worthy of being known as the properties of any other thing in the contemplation alone of which we delight. I shall, therefore, pursue the same method in considering the nature and strength of the affects and the power of the mind over them which I pursued in our previous discussion of God and the mind, and I , shall consider human actions and appetites just as if I were considering lines, planes or bodies.

DEFINITIONS

DEF. I. — I call that an **adequate cause** whose effect can be clearly and distinctly perceived by means of the cause. I call that an inadequate or partial cause whose effect cannot be understood by means of the cause alone.

DEF. II. — I say that we **act** when anything is done, either within us or without us, of which we are the adequate cause, that is to say (by the preceding Def.), when from our nature anything follows, either within us or without us, which by that nature alone can be clearly and distinctly understood. On the other hand, I say that we *suffer* when anything is done within us, or when anything follows from our nature, of which we are not the cause excepting partially.

DEF. III. — By **affect** I understand the affections of the body, by which the power of acting of the body itself is increased, diminished, helped, or hindered, together with the ideas of these affections.

If, therefore, we can be the adequate cause of any of these affections, I understand the affect to be an action, otherwise it is a passion.

Postulate 1. — The human body can be affected in many ways by which its power of acting is increased or diminished, and also in other ways which make its power of acting neither greater nor less.

Postulate 2. — The human body is capable of suffering many changes, and, nevertheless, can retain the impressions or traces of the objects and consequently the same images of things.

PROP. 1. — *Our mind acts at times and at times suffers; in so far as it has adequate ideas, it necessarily acts; and in so far as it has inadequate id as, it necessarily suffers.*

Corol, — Hence it follows that the mind is subject to passions in proportion to the number of inadequate ideas which it has, and that it acts in proportion to the number of adequate ideas which it has.

PROP. 2. — *The body cannot determine the mind to thought, neither can the mind determine the body to motion nor rest, nor anything else, if there be anything.*

Schol. — [...] The mind and the body are one and the same thing, conceived at one time under the attribute of thought, and at another under that of extension. For this reason, the order or concatenation of things is one, whether nature be conceived under this or under that attribute, and consequently the order of the actions and passions of our body is coincident in nature with the order of the actions and passions of the mind.

[...] When the body is asleep, the mind slumbers with it, and has not the power to think, as it has when the body is awake. Again, I believe that all have discovered that the mind is not always equally fitted for thinking about the same subject, but in proportion to the fitness of the body for this or that image to be excited in it will the mind be better fitted to contemplate this or that object.

[...] Human affairs would be much more happily conducted if it were equally in the power of people to be silent and to speak; but experience shows over and over again that there is nothing which people have less power over than the tongue, and that there is nothing which they are less able to do than to govern their appetites, so that many persons believe that we do those things only with freedom which we seek indifferently; as the desire for such things can easily be lessened by the recollection of another thing which we frequently call to mind; it being impossible, on the other hand, to do those things with freedom which we seek with such ardour that the recollection of another thing is unable to mitigate it.

But if, however, we had not found out that we do many things which we afterwards repent, and that when agitated by conflicting affects we see that which is better and follow that which is worse, nothing would hinder us from believing that we do everything with freedom. Thus the infant believes that it is by free will that it seeks the breast; the angry boy believes that by free will he wishes vengeance; the timid man thinks it is with free will he seeks flight; the drunkard believes that by a free command of their mind he speaks the things which when sober he wishes he had left unsaid.

Thus the madman, the chatterer, the boy, and others of the same kind, all believe that they speak by a free command of the mind, whilst, in truth, they have no power to restrain the impulse which they have to speak, so that experience itself, no less than reason, clearly teaches that people believe themselves to be free simply because they are conscious of their own actions, knowing nothing of the causes by which they are determined; it teaches, too, that the decrees of the mind are nothing but the appetites themselves, which differ, therefore, according to the different temper of the body. For every human being determines all things from their affect; those who are agitated by contrary affects do not know what they want, whilst those who are agitated by no affect are easily driven hither and thither.

All this plainly shows that the decree of the mind, the appetite, and determination of the body are coincident in nature, or rather that they are one and the same thing, which, when it is considered under the attribute of thought and explained by that, is called a decree, and when it is considered under the attribute of extension and is deduced from the laws of motion and rest, is called a determination.

This, however, will be better understood as we go on, for there is another thing which I wish to be observed here — that we cannot by a mental decree do a thing unless we recollect it. We cannot speak a word, for instance, unless we recollect it. But it is not in the free power of the mind either to recollect a thing or to forget it?

It is believed, therefore, that the power of the mind extends only thus far — that from a mental decree we can speak or be silent about a thing only when we recollect it. But when we dream that we speak, we believe that we do so from a free decree of the mind; and yet we do not speak, or, if we do, it is the result of a spontaneous motion of the body. We dream, again, that we are concealing things, and that we do this by virtue of a decree of the mind like that by which, when awake, we are silent about things we know. We dream, again, that, from a decree of the mind, we do some things which we should not dare to do when awake. And I should like to know, therefore, whether there are two kinds of decrees in the mind — one belonging to dreams and the other free.

PROP. 3. — *The actions of the mind arise from adequate ideas alone, but the passions depend upon those alone which are inadequate.*

Schol. — We see, therefore, that the passions are not related to the mind, unless in so far as it possesses something which involves negation; in other words, unless in so far as it is considered as a part of nature, which by itself and without the other parts cannot be clearly and distinctly perceived. In the same way I could show that passions are related to individual things, just as they are related to the mind, and that they cannot be perceived in any other way; but my purpose is to treat of the human mind alone.

PROP. 4. — *A thing cannot be destroyed except by an external cause.*

PROP. 5. — *In so far as one thing is able to destroy another are they of contrary natures; that is to say, they cannot exist in the same subject.*

PROP. 6. — *Each thing, in so far as it is in its endeavours to persevere in its being,*

PROP. 7. — *The effort by which each thing endeavours to persevere in its own being is nothing but the actual essence of the thing itself.*

PROP. 8. — *The effort by which each thing endeavours to persevere in its own being does not involve finite but indefinite time.*

PROP. 9. — *The mind, both in so far as it has clear and distinct ideas, and in so far as it has confused ideas endeavours to persevere in its being for an indefinite time, and is conscious of this effort.*

Schol. — This effort, when it is related to the mind alone, is called *will*, but when it is related at the same time both to the mind and the body, is called *appetite* which is therefore nothing but the very essence of human beings, from the nature of which necessarily follow those things which promote their preservation, and thus they are determined to do those things. Hence there is no difference between appetite and desire, unless in this particular, that desire is generally related to people in so far as they are conscious of their appetites, and it may therefore be defined as appetite of which we are conscious. From what has been said it is plain, therefore, that we neither strive for, wish. seek, nor desire anything because we think it to be good, but, on the contrary, we adjudge a thing to be good because we strive for, wish, seek, or desire it.

PROP. 10. — *There can be no idea in the mind which excludes the existence of the body, for such an idea is contrary to the mind.*

PROP. 11. — *If anything increases, diminishes, helps, or limits our body's power of action, the idea of that thing increases, diminishes, helps, or limits our mind's power of thought.*

Schol, — We thus see that the mind can suffer great changes, and can pass now to a greater and now to a lesser perfection; these passions explaining to us the affects of joy and sorrow. By joy, therefore, in what follows, I shall understand the passion by which the mind passes to a greater perfection; by sorrow on the other hand, the passion by which it passes to a less perfection. The affect of joy, related at the same time both to the mind and the body, I call pleasurable excitement (*titillatio*) or cheerfulness; that of sorrow I call pain or melancholy. It is, however, to be observed that pleasurable excitement and pain are related to a person when one of their parts is affected more than the others; cheerfulness and melancholy, on the other hand, when all parts are equally affected. What the nature of desire is I have explained in the scholium of Prop. 9, pt. 3; and besides these three — joy, sorrow, and desire — I know of no other primary affect, the others springing from these, as I shall show in what follows. But before I advance any farther, I should like to explain more fully Prop. 10, pt. 3, so that we may more clearly understand in what manner one idea is contrary to another.

The idea which forms the essence of the mind involves the existence of the body so long as the body exists.

PROP. 12. — *The mind endeavours as much as possible to imagine those things which increase or assist the body's power of acting.*

PROP. 13. — *Whenever the mind imagines those things which lessen or limit the body's power of action, it endeavours as much as possible to recollect what excludes the existence of these things.*

PROP. 14. — *If the mind at any time has been simultaneously affected by two affects, whenever it is afterwards affected by one of them, it will also be affected by the other.*

PROP. 15. — *Anything may be actually the cause of joy, sorrow, or desire.*

Corol. — The fact that we have contemplated a thing with an affect of joy or sorrow, of which it is not the efficient cause, is a sufficient reason for being able to love or hate it.

Schol. — We now understand why we love or hate certain things from no cause which is known to us, but merely from sympathy or antipathy, as they say. To this class, too, as we shall show in the following propositions, are to be referred those objects which affect us with joy or sorrow solely because they are somewhat like objects which usually affect us with those affects. I know indeed that the writers who first introduced the words " Sympathy" and "Antipathy" desired thereby to signify certain hidden qualities of things, but nevertheless I believe that we shall be permitted to understand by those names qualities which are plain and well known.

PROP. 16. — *If we imagine a certain thing to possess something which resembles an object which usually affects the mind with joy or sorrow, although the quality in which the thing resembles the object is not the efficient cause of these affects, we shall nevertheless, by virtue of the resemblance alone, love or hate the thing.*

PROP. 17. — *If we imagine that a thing that usually affects us with the affect of sorrow has any resemblance to an object which usually affects us equally with a great affect of joy, we shall at the same time hate the thin/j and love it.*

Schol, — This state of mind, which arises from two contrary affects, is called vacillation of the mind. It is related to affect as doubt is related to the imagination. Nor do vacillation and doubt differ from one another except. as greater and less. For the human body is composed of a number of individuals of different natures, and therefore it can be affected by one and the same body in very many and in different ways. On the other hand, the same object can be affected in a number of different ways, and consequently can affect the same part of the body in different ways. It is easy, therefore, to see how one and the same object may be the cause of many and contrary affects.

PROP. 18. — *A man is affected by the image of a past or future thing with the same affect of joy or sorrow as that with which they are affected by the image of a present thing.*

Schol. 1. — I call a thing here past or future in so far as we have been or shall be affected by it; for example, in so far as we have seen a thing or are about to see it, in so far as it has strengthened us or will strengthen us; has injured or will injure us. For in so far as we thus imagine it do we affirm its existence; that is to say, the body is affected by no affect which excludes the existence of the thing, and therefore the body is affected by the image of the thing in the same way as if the thing itself were present. But because it generally happens that those who possess much experience hesitate when they think of a thing as past or future, and doubt greatly concerning its issue, therefore the affects which spring from such images of things are not so constant, but are generally disturbed by the images of other things, until people become more sure of this issue.

Schol. 2. — From what has now been said we understand the nature of *Hope, Fear, Confidence, Despair, Gladness,* and *Remorse.* Hope is nothing but unsteady joy, arising from the image of a future or past thing about whose issue we are in doubt Fear, on the other hand, is an unsteady sorrow, arising from the image of a doubtful thing. If the doubt be removed from these objects, then hope and fear become Confidence and Despair, that is to say, joy or sorrow, arising from the image of a thing for which we have hoped or which we have feared. Gladness, again, is joy arising from the image of a past thing whose issues we have doubted. Remorse is the sorrow which is opposed to gladness.

PROP. 19. — People *who imagine that what they love is destroyed will sorrow, but if they imagine that it is preserved they will rejoice.*

PROP. 20. — People *who imagine that what they hate is destroyed will rejoice.*

PROP. 21. — People *who imagine that what they love is affected with joy or sorrow will also be affected with joy or sorrow, and these affects will be greater or less in the lover as they are greater or less in the thing loved.*

PROP. 22. — *If we imagine that a person affects with joy a thing which we love, we shall be affected with love towards them. If, on the contrary, we imagine that a person affects it with sorrow, we shall also be affected with hatred towards them.*

Schol, — Prop. 21 explains to us what *commiseration* is, which we may define as sorrow which springs from another's loss. By what name the joy is to be called which springs from another's good I do not know love toward the person who has done good to another we shall call *favour (favor)*, whilst hatred towards them who has done evil to another we shall call *indignation (indignatio)*.

PROP. 23. — *People who imagine that what they hate is affected with sorrow will rejoice; if, on the other hand, they imagine it to be affected with joy they will be sad; and these affects will be greater or less in them in proportion as their contraries are greater or less in the object they hate.*

Schol. — This joy can hardly be solid and free from any mental conflict.

PROP. 24. — *If we imagine that a person affects with joy a thing which we hate, we are therefore affected with hatred towards them. On the other hand, if we imagine that they affect it with sorrow, we are therefore affected with love towards them.*

Schol, — These and the like affects of hatred are related to *envy*, which is therefore nothing but hatred in so far as it is considered to dispose a person so that he or she rejoices over the evil and is saddened by the good which befalls another.

PROP. 25. — *We endeavour to affirm everything, both concerning ourselves and concerning the beloved object which we imagine will affect us or the object with joy, and, on the contrary, we endeavour to deny everything that will affect either it or ourselves with sorrow.*

PROP. 26. — *If we hate a thing, we endeavour to affirm concerning it everything which we imagine will affect it with sorrow, and, on the other hand, to deny everything concerning it which we imagine will affect it with joy.*

Schol. — We see from this how easily it may happen, that a person should think too much of themselves or of the beloved object, and, on the contrary, should think too little of what that person hates. When a person thinks too much of themselves, this imagination is called *pride*, and is a kind of delirium, because this person dreams with their eyes open, that they are able to do all those things to which they attain in imagination alone, regarding them therefore as realities, and rejoicing in them so long as they cannot imagine anything to exclude their existence and limit their power of action. Pride, therefore, is that joy which arises from a person's thinking too much of themselves. The joy which arises from thinking too much of another is called *over-estimation*, and that which arises from thinking too little of another is called *contempt*.

PROP. 27. — *Although we may not have been moved towards a thing by any affect, yet if it is like ourselves, whenever we imagine it to be affected by any affect we are therefore affected by the same.*

Schol. — This imitation of affects, when it is connected with sorrow, is called *commiseration*, and where it is connected with desire is called *emulation*, which is nothing else than the desire which is engendered in us for anything, because we imagine that other persons, who are like ourselves, possess the same desire.

Corol. 1. — If we imagine that a person to whom we have been moved by no affect, affects with joy a thing which is like us, we shall therefore be affected with love towards them. If, on the other hand, we imagine that that person affects it with sorrow, we shall be affected with hatred towards them.

Corol. 2. — If we pity a thing, the fact that its misery affects us with sorrow will not make us hate it.

Corol. 3. — If we pity a thing, we shall endeavour as much as possible to free it from its misery.

Schol. — This will or desire of doing good, arising from our pity for the object which we want to benefit, is called *benevolence*, which is, therefore, simply the desire which arises from commiseration.

PROP. 28. — *We endeavour to bring into existence everything which we imagine conduces to joy, and to remove or destroy everything opposed to it, or which we imagine conduces to sorrow,*

PROP. 29. — *We shall endeavour to do everything which we imagine people will look upon with joy, and, on the contrary, we shall be averse to doing anything to which we imagine people are averse.*

Schol. — This effort to do some things and omit doing others, solely because we wish to please people, is called ambition, especially if our desire to please the common people is so strong that our actions or omissions to act are accompanied with injury to ourselves or to others. Otherwise this endeavour is usually called *humanity*. Again, the joy with which we imagine another person's action, the purpose of which is to delight us, I call *praise*, and the sorrow with which we turn away from an action of a contrary kind I call *blame*.

PROP. 30. — *If a person has done anything which this person imagines will affect others with joy, he or she also will be affected with joy, accompanied with an idea of themselves as its cause; that is to say, they will look upon themselves with joy. If, on the other hand they have done anything which they imagine will affect others with sorrow, they will look upon themselves with sorrow.*

Schol, — Since love is joy attended with the idea of an external cause, and hatred is sorrow attended with the idea of an external cause, the joy and sorrow spoken of in this proposition will be a kind of love and hatred. But because love and hatred are related to external objects, we will therefore give a different name to the affects which are the subject of this proposition, and we will call this kind of joy which is attended with the idea of an external cause *self-exaltation*, and the sorrow opposed to it we will call *shame*. The reader is to understand that this is the case in which joy or sorrow arises because the person believes that they are praised or blamed, otherwise I shall call this joy accompanied with the idea of an external cause *contentment* with one's-self, and the sorrow opposed to it *repentance*. Again, since it may happen that the joy with which a person imagines that they affect other people is only imaginary, and since everyone endeavours to imagine concerning themselves what they suppose will affect themselves with joy, it may easily happen that the self-exalted person becomes proud, and imagines that they are pleasing everybody when they are offensive to everybody.

PROP. 31. — *If we imagine that a person loves, desires, or hates a thing which we ourselves love, desire, or hate, we shall on that account love, desire, or hate the thing more steadily. If, on the other hand, we imagine that they are averse to the thing we love or loves* the thing to which we are averse, we shall then suffer vacillation of mind.

Corol. — It follows from this proposition and from Prop. 28, that everyone endeavours as much as possible to make others love what they love, and to hate what they hate. Hence the poet says — "Speremus pariter, pariter metuamus amantes; Ferreus exist, si quis, quod sinit alter, amat."

This effort to make everyone approve what we love or hate is in truth ambition, and so we see that each person by nature desires that other persons should live according to their way of thinking; but if everyone does this, then all are a hindrance to one another, and if every one wishes to be praised or beloved by the rest, then they all hate one another.

PROP. 32. — *If we imagine that a person delights in a thing which only one can possess, we do all we can to prevent their possessing it.*

Schol. — We see, therefore, that the nature of human beings is generally constituted so as to pity those who are in adversity and envy those who are in prosperity, and they envy with a hatred which is the greater in proportion as they love what they imagine others possess. We see also that from the same property of human nature from which it follows that humans pity one another it also follows that they are envious and ambitious. If we will consult experience, we shall find that she teaches the same doctrine, especially if we consider the first years of our life.

PROP. 33. — *If we love a thing which is like ourselves, we endeavour as much as possible to make it love us in return.*

PROP. 34. — *The greater the affect with which we imagine that a beloved object is affected towards its, the greater will be our self-exaltation.*

PROP. 35. — *If I imagine that an object beloved by me is united to another person by the same, or by a closer bond of friendship than that by which I myself alone held the object, I shall be affected with hatred towards the beloved object itself and shall envy that other person.*

Schol, — This hatred towards a beloved object when joined with envy is called *jealousy,* which is therefore nothing but a vacillation of the mind springing from the love and hatred both felt together, and attended with the idea of another person whom we envy. Moreover, this hatred towards the beloved object will be greater in proportion to the joy with which the jealous person has been usually affected from the mutual affection between them and their beloved, and also in proportion to the affect with which they had been affected towards the person who is imagined to unite to themselves the beloved object. For if they have hated them, they will for that very reason hate the beloved object because they imagine it to affect with joy that which they hate, and also because they are compelled to connect the image of the beloved object with the image of those whom they hate.

This feeling is generally excited when the love is love towards a woman. The man who imagines that the woman he loves prostitutes herself to another is not merely troubled because their appetite is restrained, but he turns away from her because they are obliged to connect the image of a beloved object with the privy parts and with what is excremental in another man; and in addition to this, the jealous person is not received with the same favour which the beloved object formerly bestowed on them.

PROP. 36. — People *who recollect things with which they have once been delighted, desire to possess these things with every condition which existed when they were first delighted with it.*

Corol. — If, therefore, the lover discovers that one of these conditions be wanting, he or she will be sad.

Schol. — This sorrow, in so far as it is related to the absence of what we love, is called *longing*.

PROP. 37. — *The desire which springs from sorrow or joy, from hatred or love, is greater in proportion as the affect is greater.*

PROP. 38. — *If a person has begun to hate a beloved thing, so that their love to it is altogether destroyed, this person will for this very reason hate it more than he or she would have done if he or she had* never loved it, and their hatred will be in greater proportion to their previous love.

PROP. 39. — *If a person hates another he or she will endeavour to do them evil, unless they fear a greater evil will therefrom arise to themselves; and, on the other hand, a person who loves another will endeavour to do them good by the same rule.*

Schol. — By *good,* I understand here every kind of joy and everything that conduces to it; chiefly, however, anything that satisfies longing, whatever that thing may be. By *evil,* I understand every kind of sorrow, and chiefly whatever thwarts longing. For we do not desire a thing because we adjudge it to be good, but, on the contrary, we call it good because we desire it, and consequently everything to which we are averse we call evil.

Each person, therefore, according to their affect judges or estimates what is good and what is evil, what is better and what is worse, and what is the best and what is the worst, Thus, the covetous person thinks plenty of money to be the best thing and poverty the worst The ambitious person desires nothing like glory, and on the other hand dreads nothing like shame. To the envious person, again, nothing is more pleasant than the misfortune of another, and nothing more disagreeable than the prosperity of another. And so each person according to their affect judges a thing to be good or evil, useful or useless.

We notice, moreover, that this affect, by which a person is so disposed as not to will the thing that person wills, and to will that which that person does not will, is called *fear,* which may therefore be defined as that apprehension which leads a person to avoid an evil in the future by incurring a lesser evil (Prop. 28). If the evil feared is *shame*, then the fear is called modesty. If the desire of avoiding the future is restrained by the fear of another evil, so that the person does not know what he or she most wishes, then this apprehension is called *consternation,* especially if both the evils feared are very great.

PROP. 40. — *If we imagine that we are hated by another without having given them any cause for it, we shall hate them in return.*

Schol. — If we imagine that we have given just cause for the hatred, we shall then be affected with *shame*. This, however, rarely happens. This reciprocity of hatred may also arise from the fact that hatred is followed by an attempt to bring evil upon them who is hated. If, therefore, we imagine that we are hated by anyone else, we shall imagine them as the cause of some evil or sorrow, and thus we shall be affected with sorrow or apprehension accompanied with the idea of the person who hates us as a cause; that is to say, we shall hate them in return, as we have said above.

Corol. 1. — If we imagine that the person we love is affected with hatred towards us, we shall be agitated at the same time both with love and hatred. For in so far as we imagine that we are hated are we determined to hate them in return. But (by hypothesis) we love them notwithstanding, and therefore we shall be agitated both by love and hatred.

Corol. 2. — If we imagine that an evil has been brought upon us through the hatred of some person towards whom we have hitherto been moved by no affect, we shall immediately endeavour to return that evil upon them.

Schol. — The attempt. to bring evil on those we hate is called *anger*, and the attempt to return the evil inflicted on ourselves is called *vengeance*.

PROP. 41. — *If we imagine that we are loved by a person without having given any cause for the love, we shall love them in return.*

Schol. — If we imagine that we have given just cause for love, we shall pride ourselves upon it. This frequently occurs, and we have said that the contrary takes place when we believe that we are hated by another person. This reciprocal love, and consequently this attempt to do good to the person who loves us, and who endeavours to do good to us, is called *thankfulness or gratitude*, and from this we can see how much readier people are to revenge themselves than to return a benefit.

Corol. — If we imagine that we are loved by a person we hate, we shall at the same time be agitated both by love and hatred. This is demonstrated in the same way as the preceding proposition.

Schol. — If the hatred prevail, we shall endeavour to bring evil upon the person by whom we are loved. This affect is called *cruelty*, especially if it is believed that the person who loves has not given any ordinary reason for hatred.

PROP. 42. — *If, moved by love or hope of self-exaltation, we have conferred a favour upon another person, we shall be sad if we see that the favour is received with ingratitude.*

PROP. 43. — *Hatred is increased through return of hatred, but may be destroyed by love.*

PROP. 44. — *Hatred which is altogether overcome by love passes into love, and the love is therefore greater than if hatred had not preceded it.*

Schol. — Notwithstanding the truth of this proposition, no one will try to hate a thing or will wish to be affected with sorrow in order that they may rejoice the more; that is to say, no one will desire to inflict loss on themselves in the hope of recovering the loss, or to become ill in the hope of getting well, inasmuch as everyone will always try to preserve their being and to remove sorrow from themselves as much as possible. Moreover, if it can be imagined that it is possible for us to desire to hate a person in order that we may love them afterwards the more, we must always desire to continue the hatred. For the love will be the greater as the hatred has been greater, and therefore we shall always desire the hatred to be more and more increased.

PROP. 45. — *If we imagine that any one like ourselves is affected with hatred towards an object like ourselves which we love, we shall hate them.*

PROP. 46. — *If we have been affected with joy or sorrow by anyone who belongs to a class or nation different from our own, and if our joy or sorrow is accompanied with the idea of this person as its cause, under the common name of their class or nation, we shall not love or hate them merely, but the whole of the class or nation to which he or she belongs.*

PROP. 47. — *The joy which arises from our imagining that what we hate has been destroyed or has been injured is not unaccompanied with some sorrow.*

Schol. — For as often as we recollect the object, although it does not actually exist, we contemplate it as present, and the body is affected in the same way as if it were present. Therefore, so long as the memory of the object remains, we are so determined as to contemplate it with sorrow, and this determination, while the image of the object abides, is restrained by the recollection of those things which exclude the existence of the object, but is not altogether removed. Therefore we rejoice only so far as the determination is restrained, and hence it happens that the joy which springs from the misfortune of the object we hate is renewed as often as we recollect the object.

For, as we have already shown, whenever its image is excited, inasmuch as this involves the existence of the object, we are so determined as to contemplate it with the same sorrow with which we were accustomed to contemplate it when it really existed. But because we have connected with this image other images which exclude its existence, the determination to sorrow is immediately restrained, and we rejoice anew; and this happens as often as this repetition takes place.

This is the reason why we rejoice as often as we call to mind any evil that is past, and why we like to tell tales about the dangers we have escaped, since whenever we imagine any danger, we contemplate it as if it were about to be, and are so determines to fear it — a determination which is again restrained by the idea of freedom, which we connected with the idea of the danger when we were freed from it, and this idea of freedom again makes us fearless, so that we again rejoice.

PROP. 48 — *Love and hatred towards any object, for example, towards Peter, are destroyed if the joy and the sorrow which they respectively involve be joined to the idea of another cause; and they are respectively diminished in proportion as we imagine that Peter has not been their sole cause.*

PROP. 49. — *For the same reason, love or hatred towards an object we imagine to be free would be greater than towards an object which is under necessity.*

Schol. — Hence it follows that our hatred or love towards one another is greater than towards other things, because we think we are free.

PROP. 50. — *Anything may be accidentally the cause either of hope or fear.*

Schol. — Things which are accidentally the causes either of hope or fear are called good or evil omens. In so far as the omens are the cause of hope and fear are they the cause of joy or of sorrow, and consequently endeavour to use them as means to obtain those things for which we hope, or to remove them as obstacles or causes of fear. It follows, too, that our natural constitution is such that we easily believe the things we hope for, and believe with difficulty those we fear, and that we think too much of the former and too little of the latter. Thus have superstitions arisen, by which people are everywhere disquieted. I do not consider it worthwhile to go any farther, and to explain here all those vacillations of mind which arise from hope and fear, since it follows from the definition alone of these affects that hope cannot exist without fear, nor fear without hope (as we shall explain more at length in the proper place). Besides, in so far as we hope for a thing or fear it, we love it or hate it, and therefore everything which has been said about hatred and love can easily be applied to hope and fear.

PROP. 51. — *Different people may be affected by one and the same object in different ways and the same person may be affected by one and the same object in different ways at different times.*

Schol. — We thus see that it is possible for one person to love a thing and for another to hate it; for this person to fear what this person does not fear, and for the same persons to love what before they hated, and to dare to do what before they feared. Again, since each judges according to their own affect what is good and what is evil, what is better and what is worse, it follows that people may change in their judgment as they do in their affects, and hence it comes to pass that when we compare people, we distinguish them solely by the difference in their affects, calling some brave, others timid, and others by other names. For example, I shall call a person *brave* who despises an evil which I usually fear, and if, besides this, I consider the fact that their desire of doing evil to a person whom they hate or doing good to one whom they love is not restrained by that fear of evil by which I am usually restrained, I call them *audacious.*

On the other hand, the person who fears an evil which I usually despise will appear *timid*, and if, besides this, I consider that their desire is restrained by the fear of an evil which has no power to restrain me, I call them *pusillanimous;* and in this way everybody will pass judgment. Finally, from this nature of human beings and the inconstancy of their judgment, in consequence of which they often judge things from mere affect, and the things which they believe contribute to their joy or their sorrow, and which, therefore, they endeavour to bring to pass or remove, are often only imaginary — to say nothing about what we have demonstrated in the Second Part of this book about the uncertainty of things — it is easy to see that humans may often be themselves the cause of their sorrow or their joy, or of being affected with sorrow or joy accompanied with the idea of themselves as its cause, so that we can easily understand what repentance and what self-approval are. *Repentance* is sorrow accompanied with the idea of one's self as the cause, and *self-approval* is joy accompanied with the idea of one's self as the cause; and these affects are very intense because people believe themselves free (Prop. 49).

PROP. 52. — *An object which we have seen before together with other objects, or which we imagine possesses nothing which is not common to it with many other objects, we shall not contemplate so long as that which we imagine possesses something peculiar.*

Schol. — This affection of the mind or imagination of a particular thing, in so far as it alone occupies the mind, is called *astonishment,* and if it is excited by an object we dread, we call it *consternation,* because astonishment at the evil so fixes us in the contemplation of itself, that we cannot think of anything else by which we might avoid the evil. On the other hand, if the objects at which we are astonished are human wisdom, industry, or anything of this kind, inasmuch as we consider that their possessor is by so much superior to ourselves, the astonishment goes by the name of *veneration*; whilst, if the objects are human anger, envy, or anything of this sort, it goes by the name of *horror.*

Again, if we are astonished at the wisdom or industry of a person we love, then our love on that account (Prop. 12, pt. 3) will be greater, and this love, united to astonishment or veneration, we call *devotion.* In the same manner it is possible to conceive of hatred, hope, confidence, and other affects being joined to astonishment, so that more affects may be deduced than can be named by the received vocabulary.

From this we see that names have been invented for affects from common usage, rather than from accurate knowledge of them. To *astonishment* is opposed *contempt,* which is usually caused, nevertheless, by our being determined to astonishment, love, or fear towards an object either because we see that another person is astonished at, loves or fears this same object, or because at first sight it appears like other objects, at which we are astonished or which we love or fear (Prop. 15, with Corol. pt. 3, and Prop. 27, pt. 3). But if the presence of the object or a more careful contemplation of it should compel us to deny that there exists in it any cause for astonishment, love, fear, &c., then from its presence itself, the mind remains determined to think rather of those things which are not in it, than of those which are in it, although from the presence of an object the mind is accustomed to think chiefly about what is in the object.

We may also observe that as devotion springs from astonishment at a thing we love, so *derision* springs from the contempt of a thing we hate or fear, whilst *scorn* arises from the contempt of folly, as *veneration* arises from astonishment at wisdom. We may also conceive of love, hope, glory, and other affects being joined to contempt, and thus deduce other affects which also we are not in the habit of distinguishing by separate words.

PROP. 53. — *When the mind contemplates itself and its own power of acting, it rejoices, and it rejoices in proportion to the distinctness with which it imagines itself and its power of action.*

Corol. — The more a person imagines that they are praised by other people, the more is this joy strengthened; for the more a person imagines that they are praised by others, the more do they imagine that they affect others with joy accompanied by the idea of themselves as a cause, and therefore they are affected with greater joy accompanied with the idea of themselves.

PROP. 54. — *Human mind endeavours to imagine those things only which posit its power of acting.*

Prop. 55. — *When the mind imagines its own weakness it necessarily sorrows.*

Corol. — This sorrow is strengthened in proportion as the mind imagines that it is blamed by others.

Schol. — This sorrow, accompanied with the idea of our own weakness, is called *humility*, and the joy which arises from contemplating ourselves is called *self-love or self-approval*. Inasmuch as this joy recurs as often as a person contemplates their own virtues or their own power of acting, it comes to pass that everyone loves to tell of their own deeds, and to display the powers both of their body and mind; and that for this reason people become an annoyance to one another. It also follows that people are naturally envious, that is to say, they rejoice over the weaknesses of their equals and sorrow over their virtues. For whenever a person imagines their own actions they are affected with joy, and their joy is the greater in proportion as they imagine that their actions express more perfection, and they imagine them more distinctly; that is to say in proportion as they are able to distinguish them from others, and to contemplate them as individual objects.

A person's joy in contemplating themselves will therefore be greatest when he or she contemplates something in themselves which they deny of other people. For if they refer that which they affirm of themselves to the universal idea of human or of animal nature, they will not so much rejoice; on the other hand, they will be sad if they imagine that their own actions when compared with those of other people are weaker than theirs, and this sorrow they will endeavour to remove (Prop. 28), either by misinterpreting the actions of their equals, or giving as great a lustre as possible to their own. It appears, therefore, that people are by nature inclined to hatred and envy, and we must add that their education assists them in this propensity, for parents are accustomed to excite their children to follow virtue by the stimulus of honour and envy alone. But an objection perhaps may be raised that we not infrequently venerate people and admire their virtues. In order to remove this objection I will add the following Corollary.

Corol. — No one envies the virtue of a person who is not their equal.

Schol. — Since, therefore, we venerate a person because we are astonished at their wisdom and bravery, &c., this happens because (as is evident from the proposition itself) we imagine that they specially possess these virtues, and that these virtues are not common to our nature. We therefore envy them no more than we envy trees their height or lions their bravery.

PROP. 56. — *Of joy, sorrow, and desire, and consequently of every affect which either like vacillation of mind, is compounded of these, or, like love, hatred, hope, and fear, is derived from them, there are just as many kinds as there are kinds of objects by which we are affected.*

Desire is the essence itself or nature of a person in so far as this nature is conceived from its given constitution as determined towards any action (Prop. 9), and therefore as a person is affected by external causes with this or that kind of joy, sorrow, love, hatred, &c., that is to say, as their nature is constituted in this or that way, so must their desire vary and the nature of one desire differ from that of another, just as the affects from which each desire arises differ. There are as many kinds of desires, therefore, as there are kinds of joy, sorrow, love, &c., and, consequently as there are kinds of objects by which we are affected.

PROP. 57. — *The affect of one person differs from the corresponding affect of another as much as the essence of the one person differs from that of the other.*

Schol. — Hence it follows that the affects of animals which are called irrational, for after we have learnt the origin of the mind we can in no way doubt that animals feel differ from human affects as much as the nature of an animal differs from that of a person. Both the person and the horse, for example, are swayed by the lust to propagate, but the horse is swayed by equine lust and the person by that which is human. The lusts and appetites of insects, fishes, and birds must vary in the same way; and so, although each individual lives contented with its own nature and delights in it, nevertheless the life with which it is contented and its joy are nothing but the idea or soul of that individual, and so the joy of one differs in character from the joy of the other as much as the essence of the one differs from the essence of the other. Finally, it follows from the preceding proposition that the joy by which the drunkard is enslaved is altogether different from the joy which is the portion of the philosopher, — a thing I wished just to hint in passing. So much, therefore, for the affects which are related to person in so far as he or she suffers. It remains that I should say a few words about those things which are related to them in so far as they act.

PROP. LVIII/58. — *Besides the joys and sorrows which are passions, there are other affects of joy and sorrow which are related to us in so far as we act.*

PROP. 59. — *Amongst all the affects which are related to the mind in so far as it acts, there are none which are not related to joy or desire.*

Schol. — All the actions which follow from the affects which are related to the mind in so far as it thinks I ascribe to fortitude, which I divide into *strength of mind* (*animositas*) and *generosity*. By strength of mind, I mean the desire by which each person endeavours from the dictates of reason alone to preserve their own being. By generosity, I mean the desire by which from the dictates of reason alone each person endeavours to help other people and to join them to them in friendship. Those actions, therefore, which have for their aim the advantage only of the doer I ascribe to strength of mind, whilst those which aim at the advantage of others I ascribe to generosity. Temperance, therefore, sobriety, and presence of mind in danger, are a species of strength of mind, while moderation and mercy are a species of generosity.

I have now, I think, explained the principal affects and vacillations of the mind which are compounded of the three primary affects, desire, joy, and sorrow, and have set them forth through their first causes. From what has been said, it is plain that we are disturbed by external causes in a number of ways, and that, like the waves of the sea agitated by contrary winds, we fluctuate in our ignorance of our future and destiny. I have said, however, that I have only explained the principal mental complications, and not all which may exist. For by the same method which we have pursued above it would be easy to show that love unites itself to repentance, scorn, shame, &c; but I think it has already been made clear to all that the affects can be combined in so many ways, and that so many variations can arise, that no limits can be assigned to their number. It is sufficient for my purpose to have enumerated only those which are of consequence; the rest, of which I have taken no notice, being more curious than important.

There is one constantly recurring characteristic of love which I have yet to notice, and that is, that while we are enjoying the thing which we desired, the body acquires from that fruition a new disposition by which it is otherwise determined, and the images of other things are excited in it, and the mind begins to imagine and to desire other things. For example, when we imagine anything which usually delights our taste, we desire to enjoy it by eating it. But whilst we enjoy it the stomach becomes full, and the constitution of the body becomes altered.

If, therefore, the body being now otherwise disposed, the image of the food, in consequence of its being present, and therefore also the effort or desire to eat it, become more intense, then this new disposition of the body will oppose this effort or desire, and consequently the presence of the food which we desired will become hateful to us, and this hatefulness is what we call *loathing or disgust.*

As for the external affections of the body which are observed in the affects, such as trembling, paleness, sobbing, laughter, and the like, I have neglected to notice them, because they belong to the body alone without any relationship to the mind. A few things remain to be said about the definitions of the affects, and I will therefore here repeat the definitions in order, appending to them what is necessary to be observed in each.

THE AFFECTS

Definition 1. — **Desire** is the essence itself of a human being in so far as it is conceived as determined to any action by any one of their affections.

Explanation. — We have said above, in Prop. 9, that desire is appetite which is self-conscious, and that appetite is the essence itself of person in so far as it is determined to such acts as contribute to their preservation. But in the same scholium I have taken care to remark that in truth I cannot recognise any difference between human appetite and desire. For whether a person be conscious of their appetite or not, it remains one and the same appetite, and so, lest I might appear to be guilty of tautology, I have not explained desire by appetite, but have tried to give such a definition of desire as would include all the efforts of human nature to which we give the name of appetite, desire, will, or impulse.

For I might have said that desire is the essence itself of person in so far as it is considered as determined to any action; but from this definition it would not follow (Prop. 23/II) that the mind could be conscious of its desire or appetite, and therefore, in order that I might include the cause of this consciousness, it was necessary (by the same proposition) to add the words, in so far as it is conceived as determined to any action by any one of their affections. For by an affection of the human essence we understand any constitution of that essence, whether it be innate, whether it be conceived through the attribute of thought alone or of extension alone, or whether it be related to both. By the word "desire," therefore, I understand all the efforts, impulses, appetites, and volitions of a person, which vary according to their changing disposition, and not unfrequently are so opposed to one another that the person is drawn hither and thither, and knows not whither to turn.

2. Joy is a human being's passage from a less to a greater perfection.

3. Sorrow is human being's passage from a greater to a less perfection.

Explanation.—I say passage, for joy is not perfection itself. If a person were born with the perfection to which he or she passes, he or she would possess it without the affect of joy; a truth which will appear the more clearly from the affect of sorrow, which is the opposite to joy. For that sorrow consists in the passage to a less perfection, but not in the less perfection itself, no one can deny, since in so far as a person shares any perfection he or she cannot be sad. Nor can we say that sorrow consists in the privation of a greater perfection, for privation is nothing. But the affect of sorrow is a reality, and it therefore must be the reality of the passage to a lesser perfection, or the reality by which person's power of acting is diminished or limited (Prop. 11). As for the definitions of cheerfulness, pleasurable excitement, melancholy, and grief, I pass these by, because they are related rather to the body than to the mind, and are merely different kinds of joy or of sorrow.

14. Astonishment is the imagination of an object in which the mind remains fixed because this particular imagination has no connection with others.

Explanation. — That which causes the mind from the contemplation of one thing immediately to pass to the thought of another (Prop. 18) is that the images of these things are connected one with the other, and are so arranged that the one follows the other; a process which cannot be conceived when the image of the thing is new, for the mind will be held in the contemplation of the same object until other causes determine it to think of other things. The imagination, therefore, considered in itself, of a new object is of the same character as other imaginations; and for this reason I do not class astonishment among the affects, nor do I see any reason why I should do it, since this abstraction of the mind arises from no positive cause by which it is abstracted from other things, but merely from the absence of any cause by which from the contemplation of one thing the mind is determined to think other things. I acknowledge, therefore (Prop. 11), only three primitive or primary affects, those of joy, sorrow, and desire; and the only reason which has induced me to speak of astonishment is, that it has been the custom to give other names to certain affects derived from the three primitives whenever these affects are related to objects at which we are astonished. This same reason also induces me to add the definition of contempt.

5. Contempt is the imagination of an object which so little touches the mind that the mind is moved by the presence of the object to imagine those qualities which are not in it rather than those which are in it. (Prop. 52). The definitions of veneration and scorn I pass by here, because they give a name, so far as I know, to none of the affects.

6. Love is joy with the accompanying idea of an external cause.

Explanation. — This definition explains will sufficient clearness the essence of love; that which is given by some authors, who define love to be the will of the lover to unite themselves to the beloved object, expressing not the essence of love but one of its properties, and in as much as these authors have not seen with sufficient clear ness what is the essence of love, they could not have a distinct conception of its properties, and consequently their definition has by everybody been thought very obscure. I must observe, however, when I say that it is a property in a lover to will a union with the beloved object, that I do not understand by will a consent or deliberation or a free decree of the mind (for that this is a fiction we have demonstrated in Prop. 48, pt. 2), nor even a desire of the lover to unite themselves with the beloved object when it is absent, nor a desire to continue in its presence when it is present, for love can be conceived without either one or the other of these desires; but by will I understand the satisfaction that the beloved object produces in the lover by its presence, by virtue of which the joy of the lover is strengthened, or at any rate supported.

7. Hatred is sorrow with the accompanying idea of an external cause.

Explanation. — What is to be observed here will easily be seen from what has been said in the explanation of the preceding definition. (Prop, 13)

8. Inclination (*propensio*) is joy with the accompanying idea of some object as being accidentally the cause of the joy.

9. Aversion is sorrow with the accompanying idea of some object which is accidentally the cause of the sorrow. (Prop. 15)

10. Devotion is love towards an object which astonishes us.

Explanation. — That astonishment arises from the novelty of the object we have shown in Prop. 52, pt. 3. If, therefore, it should happen that we often imagine the object lit which we are astonished, we shall cease to be astonished at it, and hence we see that the affect of devotion easily degenerates into simple love.

/11. Derision is joy arising from the imagination that something we despise is present in an object we hate.

Explanation. — In so far as we despise a thing we hate do we deny its existence (Prop. 52), and so far (Prop. 20) do we rejoice. But inasmuch as we suppose that people hate what they ridicule, it follows that this joy is not solid. (Prop. 47).

12. Hope is a joy not constant, arising from the idea of something future or past, about which they are sure, of which we sometimes doubt.

13. Fear is a sorrow not constant, arising from the idea of something future or past, about this issue of which we sometimes doubt. (Prop. 18, pt. 3.)

Explanation. — From these definitions it follows that there is no hope without fear nor fear without hope, for the person who wavers in hope and doubts concerning this issue of anything is supposed to imagine something which may exclude its existence, and so far, therefore, to be sad (Prop. 19, pt. 3), and consequently while this person wavers in hope, to fear lest their wishes should not be accomplished. So also the person who fears, that is to say, who doubts whether what he or she hates will not come to pass, imagines something which excludes the existence of what he or she hates, and therefore (Prop. 20/III) rejoices, and consequently so far hopes that it will not happen.

14. Confidence is joy arising from the idea of a past or future object from which cause for doubting is removed.

X15. Despair is sorrow arising from the idea of a past or future object from which cause for doubting is removed.

Explanation. — Confidence, therefore, springs from hope and despair from fear, whenever the reason for doubting this issue is taken away; a case which occurs either because we imagine a thing past or future to be present and contemplate it as present, or because we imagine other things which exclude the existence of those which made us to doubt.

For although we can never be sure about this issue of individual objects (Corol. Prop. 31, pt. 2), it may nevertheless happen that we do not doubt it. For elsewhere we have shown (Prop. 49) that it is one thing not to doubt and another to possess certitude, and so it may happen that from the image of an object either past or future we are affected with the same affect of joy or sorrow as that by which we should be affected from the image of an object present, as we have demonstrated in Prop. 18, to which, together with the scholium, the reader is referred.

16. Gladness (*gaudium*) is joy with the accompanying idea of something past, which, unhoped for, has happened.

17. Remorse is sorrow with the accompanying idea of something past, which, unhoped for, has happened.

18. Commiseration is sorrow with the accompanying idea of evil which has happened to someone whom we imagine like ourselves.

Explanation. — Between commiseration and compassion there seems to be no difference, excepting perhaps that commiseration refers rather to an individual affect and compassion to it as a habit.

19. Favour is love towards those who have benefited others.

20. Indignation is hatred towards those who have injured others.

Explanation. — I am aware that these names in common bear a different meaning. But my object is not to explain the meaning of words but the nature of things, and to indicate them by words whose customary meaning shall not be altogether opposed to the meaning which I desire to bestow upon them. I consider it sufficient to have said this once for all.

22. Over-estimation consists in thinking too highly of another person in consequence of our love for them.

23. Contempt consists in thinking too little of another person in consequence of our hatred for them.

Explanation. — Over-estimation and contempt. are therefore respectively effects or properties of love or hatred, and so over-estimation may be defined as love in so far as it affects a person so that he or she thinks too much of the beloved object; and, on the contrary, contempt. may be defined as hatred in so far as it affects a person so that they think too little of the object they hate.

////////////////////////
people so that they are sad at the good fortune of another person and are glad when any evil happens to them.

Explanation. — To envy is generally opposed compassion (*misericordia*), which may therefore be defined as follows, notwithstanding the usual signification of the word.

I24. Compassion is love in so far as it affects people so that they are glad at the prosperity of another person and are sad when any evil happens to them.

Explanation. — These are affects of joy and sorrow which are attended by the idea of an external object as their cause, either of itself or accidentally. I pass now to consider other affects which are attended by the idea of something within as the cause.

25. Self-satisfaction is the joy which is produced by contemplating ourselves and our own power of action.

26. Humility is the sorrow which is produced by contemplating our impotence or helplessness.

Self-satisfaction is opposed to humility in so far as we understand by the former the joy which arises from contemplating our power of action, but in so far as we understand by it joy attended with the idea of something done, which we believe has been done by a free decree of our mind, it is opposed to repentance, which we may thus define —

27. Repentance is sorrow accompanied with the idea of something done which we believe has been done by a free decree of our mind.

Explanation. —Here, however, I must observe, that it is not to be wondered at that sorrow should always follow all those actions which are from custom called wicked, and that joy should follow those which are called good. But that this is chiefly the effect of education will be evident m what we have before said. Parents, by reprobating what are called bad actions, and frequently blaming their children whenever they commit them, while they persuade them to what are called good actions, and praise their children when they perform them, have caused the emotions of sorrow to connect themselves with the former, and those of joy with the latter. Experience proves this, for custom and religion are not the same everywhere; but, on the contrary, things which are sacred to some are profane to others, and what are honourable with some are disgraceful with others. Education alone, therefore, will determine whether a person will repent of any deed or boast of it.

28. Pride is thinking too much of ourselves, through self-love.

Explanation. — Pride differs, therefore, from over-estimation, inasmuch as the latter is related to an external object, but pride to the person themselves who thinks of themselves too highly. As over-estimation, therefore, is an effect or property of love, so pride is an effect or property of self-love, and it may therefore be defined as love of ourselves or self-satisfaction, in so far as it affects us so that we think too highly of ourselves.

To this affect a contrary does not exist, for no one, through hatred of themselves, thinks too little of themselves; indeed, we may say that no one thinks too little of themselves, in so far as they imagine themselves unable to do this or that thing. For whatever they imagine that they cannot do, that thing they necessarily imagine, and by their imagination are so disposed that they are actually incapable of doing what they imagine they cannot do. So long, therefore, as they imagine themselves unable to do this or that thing, so long are they not determined to do it, and consequently so long it is impossible for them to do it. If, however, we pay attention to what depends upon opinion alone, we shall be able to conceive it possible for a person to think too little of themselves, for it may happen that while they sorrowfully contemplate their own weakness they will imagine themselves despised by everybody, although nothing could be further from their thoughts than to despise them.

People may also think too little of themselves if in the present they deny something of themselves in relation to a future time of which they are not sure; for example, when they deny that they can conceive of nothing with certitude, and that they can desire and do nothing which is not wicked and base. We may also say that a person thinks too little of themselves when we see that, from an excess of fear or shame, they do not dare to do what others who are their equals dare to do. This affect, to which I will give the name of despondency, may therefore be opposed to pride; for as self-satisfaction springs from pride, so despondency springs from humility, and it may therefore be defined thus —

29. Despondency is thinking too little of ourselves through sorrow.

Explanation. — We are, nevertheless, often in the habit of opposing humility to pride, but only when we attend to their effects rather than to their nature. For we are accustomed to call a person proud who boasts too much (Prop. 30), who talks about nothing but their own virtues and other people's vices, who wishes to be preferred to everybody else, and who marches along with that stateliness and pomp which belong to others whose position is far above their own. On the other hand, we call a person humble who often blushes, who confesses their own faults and talks about the virtues of others, who yields to everyone, who walks with bended head, and who neglects to adorn themselves. These affects, humility and despondency, are very rare, for human nature, considered in itself, struggles against them as much as it can (Props. 13 and 54), and hence those who have the most credit for being abject and humble are generally the most ambitious and envious.

30. Self-exaltation is joy with the accompanying idea of some action we have done, which we imagine people praise.

31. Shame is sorrow, with the accompanying idea of some action which we imagine people blame.

Explanation. —A difference is here to be observed between shame and modesty. Shame is sorrow which follows a deed of which we are ashamed. Modesty is the dread or fear of shame, which keeps a person from committing any disgraceful act. To modesty is usually opposed impudence, which indeed is not an affect, as I shall show in the proper place; but the names of affects, as I have already said, are matters rather of custom than indications of the nature of the affects. I have thus discharged the task which I set myself of explaining the affects of joy and sorrow. I will advance now to those which I ascribe to desire.

32. Regret is the desire or longing to possess something, the affect being strengthened by the memory of the object itself, and at the same time being restrained by the memory of other things which exclude the existence of the desired object.

Explanation. — Whenever we recollect a thing, as we have often said, we are thereby necessarily disposed to contemplate it with the same affect as if it were present before us. But this disposition or effort, while we are awake, is generally restrained by the images of things which exclude the existence of the thing which we recollect. Whenever, therefore, we recollect a thing which affects us with any kind of joy, we thereby endeavour to contemplate it with the same affect of joy as if it were present, — an attempt. which is, however, immediately restrained by the memory of that which excludes the existence of the thing. Regret, therefore, is really a sorrow which is opposed to the joy which arises from the absence of what we hate. (Prop. 47). But because the name regret seems to connect this affect with desire, I therefore ascribe it to desire.

33. Emulation is the desire which is begotten in us of a thing because we imagine that other persons have the same desire.

Explanation. — People who seek flight because others seek it, they who fear because they see others fear, or even they who withdraw their hands and moves their body as if their hands were burning because they see that another person has burnt their hand, such as these, I say, although they may indeed imitate the affect of another, are not said to emulate it; not because we have recognised one cause for emulation and another for imitation, but because it has been the custom to call that person only emulous who imitates what we think noble, useful, or pleasant.

34. Thankfulness or **gratitude** is the desire or endeavour of love with which we strive to do good to others who, from a similar affect of love, have done good to us (Prop. 39, 41).

X35. Benevolence is the desire to do good to those whom we pity.

36. Anger is the desire by which we are impelled, through hatred, to injure those whom we hate (Prop. 39).

37. Vengeance is the desire which, springing from mutual hatred, urges us to injure those who, from a similar affect, have injured us.

38. Cruelty or ferocity is the desire by which people are impelled to injure any one whom they love or pity.

Explanation. — To cruelty is opposed mercy, which is not a passion, but a power of the mind by which a person restrains anger and vengeance.

39. Fear is the desire of avoiding the greater of two dreaded evils by the less.

40. Audacity is the desire by which we are impelled to do something which is accompanied with a danger which our equals fear to meet.

41. A person is said to be **pusillanimous** whose desire is restrained by the fear of a danger which their equals dare to meet.

Explanation. — Pusillanimity, therefore, is nothing but the dread of some evil which most persons do not usually fear, and therefore I do not ascribe it to the affects of desire. I wished, notwithstanding, to explain it here, because in so far as we attend to desire, pusillanimity is the true opposite of the affect of audacity.

42. Consternation is affirmed of the person whose desire of avoiding evil is restrained by astonishment at the evil which he or she fears.

Explanation. — Consternation is therefore a kind of pusillanimity. But because consternation springs from a double fear, it may be more aptly defined as that dread which holds a person stupefied or vacillating, so that he or she cannot remove an evil. I say stupefied, in so far as we understand their desire of removing the evil to be restrained by their astonishment. I say also vacillating, in so far as we conceive the same desire to be restrained by the fear of another evil which equally tortures them, so that they do not know which of the two evils to avoid.

43. Courtesy or moderation is the desire of doing those things which please people and omitting those which displease them.

XLI44. Ambition is the immoderate desire of glory.

Explanation. — Ambition is a desire which increases and strengthens all the affects (Props. 27 and 31), and that is the reason why it can hardly be kept under control. For so long as a person is possessed by any desire, they are necessarily at the same time possessed by this. Every noble person, says Cicero, is led by glory, and even the philosophers who write books about despising glory place their names on the title-page.

45. Luxuriousness is the immoderate desire or love of good living.

46. Drunkenness is the immoderate desire and love of drinking.

47. Avarice is the immoderate desire and love of riches.

48. Lust is the immoderate desire and love of sexual intercourse.

Explanation. — This desire of sexual intercourse is usually called lust, whether it be held within bounds or not. I may add that the five last-mentioned affects have no contraries, for moderation is a kind of ambition, and I have already observed that temperance, sobriety, and chastity show a power and not a passion of the mind.

Even supposing that an avaricious, ambitious, or timid person refrains from an excess of eating, drinking, or sexual intercourse, avarice, ambition, and fear are not therefore the opposites of voluptuousness, drunkenness, or lust. For the avaricious person generally desires to swallow as much meat and drink as he or she can, provided only it belongs to another person. The ambitious person, too, if he or she hopes they can keep it a secret, will restrain themselves in nothing, and if he lives amongst drunkards and libertines, will be more inclined to their vices just because they are ambitious. The timid person, too, does what he or she does not will; and although, in order to avoid death, he or she may throw their riches into the sea, he or she remains avaricious; nor does the lascivious person cease to be lascivious because they are sorry that he or she cannot gratify their desire. Absolutely, therefore, these affects have reference not so much to the acts themselves of eating and drinking as to the appetite and love itself. Consequently nothing can be opposed to these affects but nobility of soul and strength of mind, as we shall see afterwards.

The definitions of jealousy and the other vacillations of the mind I pass over in silence, both because they are compounded of the affects which we have already defined, and also because many of them have no names — a fact which shows that, for the purposes of life, it is sufficient to know these combinations generally. Moreover, it follows from the definitions of the affects which we have explained that they all arise from desire, joy, or sorrow, or rather that there are none but these three, which pass under names varying as their relations and external signs vary. If, therefore, we attend to these primitive affects and to what has been said above about the nature of the mind, we shall be able here to define the affects in so far as they are related to the mind alone.

General definition of the affects. — **Affect,** which is called *anima pathema,* is a confused idea by which the mind affirms of its body, or any part of it, a greater or less power of existence than before; and this increase of power being given, the mind itself is determined to one particular thought rather than to another.

Explanation. — I say, in the first place, that an affect or passion of the mind is a confused idea. For we have shown (Prop. 3) that the mind suffers only in so far as it has inadequate or confused ideas. *I say again, by which the mind affirms of its body, or any part of it, a greater or less power of existence than before.* For all ideas which we possess of bodies indicate the actual constitution of our body rather than the nature of the external body; but this idea, which constitutes the form of an affect, must indicate or express the constitution of the body, or of some part of it; which constitution the body or any part of it possesses from the fact that its power of action or force of existence is increased or diminished, helped or limited.

But it is to be observed, that when I say *a greater or less power of existence than before*, I do not mean that the mind compares the present with the past constitution of the body, but that the idea which constitutes the form of affect affirms something of the body which actually involves more or less reality than before. Moreover, since the essence of the mind (Props. 11 and 13) consists in its affirmation of the actual existence of its body, and since we understand by perfection the essence itself of the thing, it follows that the mind passes to a greater or less perfection when it is able to affirm of its body, or some part of it, something which involves a greater or less reality than before. When, therefore, I have said that the mind's power of thought is increased or diminished, I have wished to be understood as meaning nothing else than that the mind has formed an idea of its body, or some part of its body, which expresses more or less reality than it had hitherto affirmed of the body. For the value of ideas and the actual power of thought are measured by value of the object.

Finally, I added, *which being given, the mind itself is determined to one particular thought rather than to another,* that I might also express the nature of desire in addition to that of joy and sorrow, which is explained by the first part of the definition.

―――――――――

END OF THE THIRD PART

ETHICS
AN OUTLINE

Fourth Part

OF HUMAN BONDAGE OR OF THE STRENGTH OF THE AFFECTS

OF HUMAN BONDAGE OR OF THE STRENGTH OF THE AFFECTS

PREFACE

The impotence of person to govern or restrain the affects I call *bondage*, for a person who is under their control is not their own master, but is mastered by fortune, in whose power they are, so that they are often forced to follow the worse, although they see the better before them. I propose in this part to demonstrate why this is, and also to show what of good and evil the affects possess.

But before I begin I should like to say a few words about perfection and imperfection, and about good and evil. If a person has proposed to do a thing and has accomplished it, he or she calls it perfect, and not only they do so, but everyone else who has really known or has believed that they have known the mind and intention of the author of that work will call it perfect too. For example, having seen some work (which I suppose to be as yet not finished), if we know that the intention of the author of that work is to build a house, we shall call the house imperfect; while, on the other hand, we shall call it perfect as soon as we see the work has been brought to the end which the author had determined for it.

But if we see any work such as we have never seen before, and if we do not know the mind of the workman, we shall then not be able to say whether the work is perfect or imperfect.[2] This seems to have been the first signification of these words; but afterwards people began to form universal ideas, to think out for themselves types of houses, buildings, castles, and to prefer some types of

---

[2] A translation cannot show the etymology of the word "perfect" as it is shown in the original Latin, so that this passage may perhaps seem rather obscure. It is only necessary, however, to bear in mind that *perfect* and *accomplished* are expressible b the same word in Latin, and that *accomplish* is the primary moaning of *perficere*, — Trans.

things to others; and so it happened that each person called a thing perfect which seemed to agree with the universal idea which he or she had formed of that thing, and, on the other hand, they called a thing imperfect which seemed to agree less with their typal conception, although, according to the intention of the workman, it had been entirely completed. This appears to be the only reason why the words *perfect* and *imperfect* are commonly applied to natural objects which are not made with human hands; for people are in the habit of forming, both of natural as well as of artificial objects, universal ideas which they regard as types of things, and which they think nature has in view, setting them before herself as types too; it being the common opinion that she does nothing except for the sake of some end.

When, therefore, people see something done by nature which does not altogether answer to that typal conception which they have of the thing, they think that nature herself has failed or committed an error, and that she has left the thing imperfect, Thus, we see that the custom of applying the words *perfect* and *imperfect* to natural objects has arisen rather from prejudice than from true knowledge of them. For we have shown in the Appendix to the First Part of this work that nature does nothing for the sake of an end, for that eternal and infinite Being whom we call God or Nature acts by the same necessity by which God exists; for we have shown that God acts by the same necessity of nature as that by which God exists (Prop. 16/I). The reason or cause, therefore, why God or nature acts and the reason why God exists are one and the same. Since, therefore, God exists for no end, God acts for no end; and since God has no principle or end of existence, God has no principle or end of action. A final cause, as it is called, is nothing, therefore, but human desire, in so far as this is considered as the principle or primary cause of anything.

For example, when we say that the having a house to live in was the final cause of this or that house, we merely mean that a person, because they imagined the advantages of a domestic life, desired to build a house. Therefore, having a house to live in, in so far as it is considered as a final cause, is merely this particular desire, which is really an efficient cause, and is considered as primary, because people are usually ignorant of the causes of their desires; for, as I have often said, we are conscious of our actions and desires, but ignominy of the causes by which we are determined to desire anything. As for the vulgar opinion that nature sometimes fails or commits an error, or produces imperfect things, I class it amongst those fictions mentioned in the Appendix to the First Part.

Perfection, therefore, and imperfection are really only modes of thought; that is to say, notions which we are in the habit of forming from the comparison with one another of individuals of the same species or genus, and this is the reason why I have said, in Def. 6/II, that by *reality* and *perfection* I understand the same thing; for we are in the habit of referring all individuals in nature to one genus, which is called the most general; that is to say, to the notion of being, which embraces absolutely all the individual objects in nature. In so far, therefore, as we refer the individual objects in nature to this genus, and compare them one with another, and discover that some possess more being or reality than others, in so far do we call some more perfect than others; and in so far as we assign to the latter anything which, like limitation, termination, impotence, &c., involves negation, shall we call them imperfect, because they do not affect our minds so strongly as those we call perfect, but not because anything which really belongs to them is wanting, or because nature has committed an error. For nothing belongs to the nature of anything excepting that which follows from the necessity of the nature of the efficient cause, and whatever follows from the necessity of the nature of the efficient cause necessarily happens.

With regard to *good* and *evil,* these terms indicate nothing positive in things considered in themselves, nor are they anything else than modes of thought, or notions which we form from the comparison of one thing with another. For one and the same thing may at the same time be both good and evil or indifferent. Music, for example, is good to a melancholy person, bad to one mourning, while to a deaf person it is neither good nor bad. But although things are so, we must retain these words. For since we desire to form for ourselves an idea of person upon which we may look as a model of human nature, it will be of service to us to retain these expressions in the sense I have mentioned. By good, therefore, I understand in the following pages everything which we are certain is a means by which we may approach nearer and nearer to the model of human nature we set before us By evil, on the contrary, I understand everything which we are certain hinders us from reaching that model.

Again, I shall call people more or less perfect or imperfect in so far as they approach more or less nearly to this same model. For it is to be carefully observed, that when I say that an individual passes from a less to a greater perfection and *vice versa*, I do not understand that from one essence or form they are changed into another (for a horse, for instance, would be as much destroyed if it were changed into a person as if it were changed into an insect), but rather we conceive that their power of action, in so far as it is understood by their own nature, is increased or diminished.

Finally, by perfection generally, I understand, as I have said, reality; that is to say, the essence of any object in so far as it exists and acts in a certain manner, no regard being paid to its duration. For no individual thing can be said to be more perfect because of a longer time it has persevered in existence; inasmuch as the duration of things cannot be determined by their essence, the essence of things involving no fixed or determined period of existence; any object, whether it be more or less perfect, always being able to persevere in existence with the same force as that with which it commenced existence. All things, therefore, are equal in this respect.

DEFINITIONS

I. — By **good**, I understand that which we certainly know is useful to us.

II. By **evil**, on the contrary, I understand that which we certainly know hinders us from possessing anything that is good.

With regard to these two definitions, see the close of the preceding preface.

III. I call individual things **contingent** in so far as we discover nothing, whilst we attend to their essence alone, which necessarily posits their existence or which necessarily excludes it.

IV. I call these individual things **possible**, in so far as we are ignorant, whilst we attend to the causes from which they must be produced, whether these causes are determined to the production of these things. In Prop. 33, I made no difference between possible and contingent, because there was no occasion there to distinguish them accurately.

V. By **contrary affects**, I understand in the following pages those which, although they may be of the same kind, draw a person in different directions; such as voluptuousness and avarice, which are both a species of love, and are not contrary to one another by nature, but only by accident.

VI. What I understand by **affect towards a thing future, present, and past**, I have explained in Prop. 18, to which the reader is referred.

Here, however, it is to be observed that it is the same with time as it is with place; for as beyond a certain limit we can form no distinct imagination of distance — that is to say, as we usually imagine all objects to be equally distant from us, and as if they were on the same plane, if their distance from us exceeds 200 feet, or if their distance from the position we occupy is greater than we can distinctly imagine — so we imagine all objects to be equally distant from the present time, and refer them as if to one moment, if the period to which their existence belongs is separated from the present by a longer interval than we can usually imagine distinctly.

VII. By end for the sake of which we do anything, I understand **appetite.**

VIII. By **virtue and power,** I understand the same thing; that is to say (Prop. 7, pt. 3), virtue, in so far as it is related to person, is the essence itself or nature of the person in so far as it has the power of effecting certain things which can be understood through the laws of its nature alone.

AXIOM

There is no individual thing in nature which is not surpassed in strength and power by some other thing, but any individual thing being given, another and a stronger is also given, by which the former can be destroyed.

PROP. 1. — *Nothing positive contained in a false idea is removed by the presence of the truth in so far as it is true.*

Schol. — [...] We know that when we groundlessly fear any evil, the fear vanishes when we hear correct intelligence; but we also know, on the other hand, that when we fear an evil which will actually come upon us, the fear vanishes when we hear false intelligence, so that the imaginations do not disappear with the presence of the truth, in so far as it is true, but because other imaginations arise which are stronger, and which exclude the present existence of the objects we imagine

PROP. 2. — *We suffer in so far as we are a part of nature which part cannot be conceived by itself nor without the other parts.*

PROP. 4. — *It is impossible that people should not be a part of nature, and that they should suffer no changes but those which can be understood through their own nature alone, and of which they are the adequate cause.*

Corol. — Hence it follows that a person is necessarily always subject to passions, and that they follow and obey the common order of nature, accommodating themselves to it as far as the nature of things requires.

PROP. 5. — *The force and increase of any passion and its perseverance in existence are not limited by the power by which we endeavour to persevere in existence but by the power of an external cause compared with our own power.*

PROP. 6. — *The other actions or power of a human being may be so far surpassed by force of some passion or affect, that the affect may obstinately cling to them.*

PROP. 7. — *An affect cannot be retrained nor removed unless by an opposed and stronger affect.*

Corol. — An affect, in so far as it is related to the mind, cannot be restrained nor removed unless by the idea of a bodily affection opposed to that which we suffer and stronger than it. For the affect which we suffer cannot be restrained nor removed unless by an opposed and stronger affect (Prop. 7, pt. 4); that is to say (by the general definition of the affects), it cannot be removed unless by the idea of a bodily affection stronger than that which affects us, and opposed to it.

PROP. 8. — *Knowledge of good or evil is nothing but an affect of joy or sorrow in so far as we arc conscious of it.*

PROP. 9. — *If we imagine the cause of an affect to be actually present with us, that affect will be stronger than if we imaging the cause not to be present.*

Corol. — The image of a past or future object, that is to say, of an object which we contemplate in relation to the past or future to the exclusion of the present, other things being equal, is weaker than the image of a pre sent object, and consequently the affect towards a future or past object, other things being equal, is weaker then than the affect towards a present object.

PROP. 10. — *We are affected with regard to a future object which we imagine will soon be present more powerfully than if we imagine that the time at which it will exist is further removed from the present, and the memory of an object which we imagine has but just passed away also affects us more powerfully than if we imagine the object to have passed away some time ago.*

Schol. — It follows that all objects which are separated from the present time by a longer interval than our imagination has any power to determine affect us equally slightly, although we know them to be separated from one another by a large space of time.

PROP. 11. — *The affect towards an object which we imagine as necessary, other things being equal, is stronger than that towards an object that is possible, contingent, or not necessary.*

PROP. 12. — *The affect towards an object which we know does not exist in the present and which we imagine as possible, other things being equal, is stronger than the affect towards a contingent object.*

Corol. — The affect towards an object which we know does not exist in the present, and which we imagine as contingent, is much weaker than if we imagined that the object were present to us.

PROP. 13. — The *affect towards a contingent object which we know does not exist in the present, other things being equal, is much weaker than the affect towards a past object.*

PROP. 14. — *No affect can be restrained by the true knowledge of good and evil in so far as it is true, but only in so far as it is considered as an affect.*

PROP. 15. — *Desire which arises from a true knowledge of good and evil can be extinguished or restrained by many other desires which take their origin from the affects by which we are agitated.*

PROP. 16. — *The desire which springs from a knowledge of good and evil can be easily extinguished or restrained, in so far as this knowledge is connected with the future, by the desire of things which in the present are sweet.*

PROP. 17. — *The desire which springs from a true knowledge of good and evil can be still more easily restrained, in so far as this knowledge is connected with objects which are contingent, by the desire of objects which are present.*

Schol. — In these propositions I consider that I have explained why people are more strongly influenced by an opinion than by true reason, and why the true knowledge of good and evil causes disturbance in the mind, and often gives way to every kind of lust, whence the saying of the poet, "*Video proboque, deteriora sequor.*"

The same thought appears to have been in the mind of the Preacher when he said, "*He that increaseth knowledge increaseth sorrow.*"

I say these things not because I would be understood to conclude, therefore, that it is better to be ignorant than to be wise, or that the wise person in governing their passions is nothing better than the fool, but I say them because it is necessary for us to know both the strength and weakness of our nature, so that we may determine what reason can do and what it cannot do in governing our affects. This, moreover, let it be remembered, is the Part in which I meant to treat of human weakness alone, all consideration of the power of reason over the passions being reserved for a future portion of the book.

PROP. 18. — *The desire which springs from joy, other things being equal, is stronger than that which springs from sorrow.*

Schol.— I have thus briefly explained the causes of human impotence and want of stability, and why people do not obey the dictates of reason. It remains for me now to show what it is which reason prescribes to us, which affects agree with the rules of human reason, and which, on the contrary, are opposed to these rules. Before, however, I begin to demonstrate these things by our full geometrical method, I should like briefly to set forth here these dictates of reason, in order that what I have in my mind about them may be easily comprehended by all.

Since reason demands nothing which is opposed to nature, it demands, therefore, that every person should love themselves, should seek their own profit, — what is truly profitable to them, — should desire everything that really leads person to greater perfection, and absolutely that everyone should endeavour, as far as in them lies, to preserve their own being. This is all true as necessarily as that the whole is greater than its part (Prop. 6, pt. 3). Again. since virtue (Def. 8, pt. 4) means nothing but acting according to the laws of our own nature, and since no one endeavours to preserve their being (Prop. 7, pt. 3) except. 1n accordance with the laws of their own nature, it follows;

Firstly, That the foundation of virtue is that endeavour itself to preserve our own being, and that happiness consists in this — that a person can preserve their own being. *Secondly,* It follows that virtue is to the desired for its own sake, nor is there anything more excellent or more useful to us than virtue, for the sake of which virtue ought to be desired.

Thirdly, It follows that all persons who kill themselves are impotent in mind, and have been thoroughly overcome by external causes opposed to their nature. Again, from Post. 4, it follows that we can never free our-selves from I lie need of something outside us for the preservation of our being, and that we can never live in such a manner as to have no intercourse with objects which are outside us. Indeed, so far as the mind is concerned, our intellect would be less perfect if the mind were alone, and understood nothing but itself. There are many things, therefore, outside us which are useful to us, and which, therefore, are to be sought.

Of all these, none more excellent can be discovered than those which exactly agree with our nature. If, for example, two individuals of exactly the same nature are joined together, they make up a single individual, doubly stronger than each alone. Nothing, therefore, is more useful to person than person. lien can desire, I say, nothing more excellent for the preservation of their being than that all should so agree at every point that the minds and bodies of all should form, as it were, one mind and one body; that all should together endeavour as much as possible to preserve their being, and that all should together seek the common good of all. From this it follows that people who are governed by reason, — that is to say, people who, under the guidance of reason, seek their own profit, — desire nothing for themselves which they do not desire for other people, and that, therefore, they are just, faithful, and honourable.

These are those dictates of reason which I purposed briefly to set forth before commencing their demonstration by a fuller method, in order that, if possible, I might win the attention of those who believe that this principle, — that everyone is bound to seek their own profit, — is the foundation of impiety, and not of virtue and piety. Having now briefly shown that this belief of their is the contrary of the truth, I proceed, by the same method as that which we have hitherto pursued, to demonstrate what I have said.

PROP. 19. — *According to the laws of their own nature each person necessarily desires that which he or she considers to be good, and avoids that which he or she considers to be evil.*

PROP. 20. — *The more each person strives and is able to seek their own profit, that is to say, to preserve their being, the more virtue does he or she possess; on the other hand, in so far as each person neglects their own profit, that is to say, neglects to preserve their own being, are they impotent.*

Schol. — No one, therefore, unless defeated by external causes and those which are contrary to their nature, neglects to seek their own profit or preserve their being. No one, I say, refuses food or kills themselves from a necessity of their nature, but only when forced by external causes. The compulsion may be exercised in many ways. A person kills themselves under compulsion by another when that other turns the right hand, with which the person had by chance laid hold of a sword, and compels them to direct the sword against their own heart; or the command of a tyrant may compel a person, as it did Seneca, to open their own veins, that is to say, they may desire to avoid a greater evil by a less.

External and hidden causes also may so dispose their imagination and may so affect their body as to cause it to put on another nature contrary to that which it had at first, and one whose idea cannot exist in the mind (Prop. 10, pt. 3); but a very little reflection will show that it is as impossible that a person, from the necessity of their nature, should endeavour not to exist, or to be changed into some other form, as it is that something should be begotten from nothing.

PROP. 21. — *No one can desire to be happy, to act well and live well, who does not at the same time desire to be, to act, and to live, that is to say, actually to exist.*

PROP. 22. — *No virtue can be conceived prior to this {the endeavour, namely, after self-preservation).*

Corol. — The endeavour after self-preservation is the primary and only foundation of virtue. For prior to this principle no other can be conceived (Prop. 22, pt. 4), and without it (Prop. 21, pt. 4) no virtue can be conceived.

PROP. 23. — *In so far as human beings are determined to any action because they have inadequate ideas, they cannot be absolutely said to act in conformity with virtue but only in so far as they are determined because they understand.*

PROP. 24. — *To act absolutely in conformity with virtue is, in us, nothing but acting, living, and preserving our being (these three things have the same meaning) as reason directs, from the ground of seeking our own profit.*

PROP. 25. — *No one endeavours to preserve their own being for the sake of another object.*

PROP. 26. — *All efforts which we make through reason are nothing but efforts to understand and the mind, in so far as it uses reason, adjudges nothing as profitable to itself excepting that which conduces to understanding.*

PROP. 27 — *We do not know that anything is certainly good or evil excepting that which actually conduces to understanding, or which can prevent us from understanding.*

PROP. 28. — *The highest good of thee mind is the knowledge of God, and the highest virtue of the mind is to know God.*

PROP. 29. — *No individual object whose nature is altogether different from our own can either help or restrain our power of acting, and absolutely nothing can be to us either good or evil unless it possesses something in common with ourselves.*

PROP. 30. — *Nothing can be evil through that which it possesses in common with our nature, but in so far as a thing is evil to us it is it contrary to its.*

PROP. 31. — *In so far as an object agrees with our nature is it necessarily good.*

Corol.— Hence it follows that the more an object agrees with our own nature, the more profitable it is to us, that is to say, the better it is for us, and, conversely, the more profitable an object is to us, the more does it agree with our own nature. For in so far as it does not agree with our nature it will necessarily be either diverse fn.)m our nature or contrary to it If diverse, it can (Prop. 29) be neither good nor evil, but if contrary, it will therefore be contrary also to that which agrees with our own nature, that is to say (Prop. 31), contrary to the good, or, in other words, it will be evil. Nothing, therefore, can be good except. 1n so far as it agrees with our nature, and therefore the more an object agrees with our nature the more profitable it will be, and *vice versa*.

PROP. 32. — *If so far as people are subject to passions, they cannot be said to agree in nature.*

PROP. 33. — *People may differ in nature from one another in so far as they are abated by affects which are passions, and in so far also as one and the same person is agitated by passions is he or she changeable and inconstant.*

PROP. 34. — *In so far as people are agitated by affects which are passions can they be contrary to one another.*

PROP. 35. — *So far as people live in conformity with the guidance of reason, in so far only do they always agree in nature.*

Corol. 1. — There is no single thing in nature which is more profitable to human beings than a person who lives according to the guidance of reason. For that is most profitable to person which most agrees with their own nature (Prop. 31), that is to say, person (as is self-evident). But a person acts absolutely from the laws of their own nature when he or she lives according to the guidance of reason (Def. 2, pt. 3), and so far only does the person always necessarily agree with the nature of another person (Prop. 35, pt. 4); therefore there is no single thing more profitable to a person than another person, &c. — Q.E.D.

Corol. 2. — When each person seeks most that which is profitable to themselves, then are people most profitable to one another; for the more each person seeks their own profit and endeavours to preserve themselves, the more virtue does he or she possess (Prop. 20), or, in other words (Def. 8), the more power does he or she possess to act according to the laws of their own nature, that is to say (Prop. 3), to live according to the guidance of reason. But people most agree in nature when they live according to the guidance of reason (Prop. 33), therefore (by the previous Corol.) people will be most profitable to one another when each person seeks most what is profitable to themselves. — Q.E.D.

Schol. — To what we have just demonstrated daily experience itself testifies by so many and such striking proofs, that it is in almost everybody's mouth that a human being is a God to another human. It is very seldom indeed that men live according to the guidance of reason; on the contrary, it so happens that they are generally envious and injurious to one another. But, nevertheless, they are scarcely ever able to lead a solitary life, so that to most people the definition of man that they are a social animal entirely commends itself, and indeed it is the case that far more advantages than disadvantages arise from the common society of human beings.

Let satirists therefore scoff at human affairs as much as they please, let theologians denounce them, and let the melancholy praise as much as they can a life rude and without refinement, despising people and admiring animals (brutes), people will nevertheless find out that by mutual help they can much more easily pro cure the things they need, and that it is only by their united strength they can avoid the dangers which every where threaten them, to say nothing about its being far nobler and worthier of our knowledge to meditate upon the doings of people than upon those of animals.

PROP. 36. — *The highest good of those who follow after virtue is common to all, and all may equally enjoy it.*

Schol. — If anybody asks, What if the highest good of those who follow after virtue were not common to all? would it not thence follow (as above, Prop. 34) that people who live according to the guidance of reason, that is to say (Prop. 35), people in so far as they agree in nature, would be contrary to one another? We reply that it arises from no accident, but from the nature itself of reason, that the highest good of human beings is common to all, inasmuch as it is deduced from the human essence itself, in so far as it is determined by reason, and also because people could not be nor be conceived if they had not the power of rejoicing in this highest good. For it pertains (Prop. 47) to the essence of the human mind to have an adequate knowledge of the eternal and infinite essence of God.

PROP. 37. — *The good which everyone who follows after virtue seeks for themselves, he or she will desire for other people; and their desire on their behalf will be greater in proportion as they have a greater knowledge of God.*

Schol. 1. — A person who strives from an affect alone to make others love what he or she themselves loves, and to make others live according to their way of thinking, acts from mere impulse, and is therefore hateful, especially to those who have other tastes, and who therefore also desire, and by the same impulse strive to make others live according to their way of thinking. Again, since the highest good which people seek from an affect is often such that only one person can possess it, it follows that persons who love are not consistent with themselves, and, whilst they delight to recount the praises of the beloved object, fear lest they should be believed. But he or she who endeavours to lead others by reason does not act from impulse, but with humanity and kindness, and is always consistent with themselves.

Everything which we desire and do, of which we are the cause in so far as we possess an idea of God, or in so far as we know God, I refer to *Religion*. The desire of doing well which is born in us, because we live according to the guidance of reason, I call Piety. The desire to join others in friendship to themselves, with which a person
living according to the guidance of reason is possessed, I call *Honour*. I call that thing Honourable which people who live according to the guidance of reason praise; and that thing, on the contrary, I call *Base* which sets itself against the formation of friendship. Moreover, I have also shown what are the foundations of a *State*.

The difference also between true virtue and impotence may, from what has already been said, be easily seen to be this — that true virtue consists in living according to the guidance of reason alone;

and that impotence therefore consists in this alone — that a person allows themselves to be led by things which are outside themselves, and by them to be determined to such actions as the common constitution of external things demands, and not to such as their own nature considered in itself alone demands. These are the things which I promised in Schol. Prop. 18, pt. 4, I would demonstrate. From them we see that the law against killing animals is based upon an empty superstition and womanish tenderness, rather than upon sound reason. The law, indeed, of seeking one's own profit teaches us to unite in friendship with people, and not with animals, nor with things whose nature is different from human nature. It teaches us, too, that the same right which they have over us we have over them. Indeed, since the right of any person is limited by their virtue or power, men possess a far greater right over animals than animals possess over people. I by no means deny that animals feel, but I do deny that on this account it is unlawful for us to consult our own profit by using them for our own pleasure and treating them as is most convenient for us, in as much as they do not agree in nature with us, and their affects are different from our own (Schol. Prop. 57, pt. 3).

It now remains that I should explain what are *Justice, Injustice, Crime*, and, finally, *Merit.*

Schol. 2. — In the Appendix to the First Part I promised I would explain what are praise and blame, merit and crime, justice and injustice. I have already shown what is the meaning of praise and blame in Schol. Prop. 29, pt. 3, and this will be a fitting place for the explanation of the rest. A few words must, however, first be said about the natural and civil state of people.

It is by the highest right of nature that each person exists, and consequently it is by the highest right of nature that each person does those things which follow from the necessity of their nature; and therefore it is by the highest right of nature that each person judges what is good and what is evil, consults their own advantage as he or she thinks best (Props. 19 and 20), avenges themselves (Prop. 40), and endeavours to preserve what they love and to destroy what they hate (Prop. 28). If people lived according to the guidance of reason, everyone would enjoy this right without injuring anyone else (Prop. 35). But because people are subject to affects (Prop. 4), which far surpass human power or virtue (Prop. 6), they are often drawn in different directions (Prop. 33), and are contrary to one another (Prop. 34), although they need one another's help (Prop. 35).

In order, then, that people may be able to live in harmony and be a help to one another, it is necessary for them to cede their natural right, and beget confidence one in the other that they will do nothing by which one can injure the other. In what manner this can be done, so that people who are necessarily subject to affects (Prop. 4), and are uncertain and changeable (Prop. 33), can beget confidence one in the other and have faith in one another, is evident from Props. 7 and 39. It is there shown that no affect can be restrained unless by a stronger and contrary affect, and that every one abstains from doing an injury through fear of a greater injury.

By this law, therefore, can society be strengthened, if only it claims for itself the right which every individual possesses of avenging themselves and deciding what is good and what is evil, and provided, therefore, that it possess the power of prescribing a common rule of life, of promulgating laws and supporting them, not by reason, which cannot restrain the affects (Prop. 17), but by penalties.

This society, firmly established by law and with a power of self-preservation, is called a *State*, and those who are protected by its right are called *Citizens*. We can now easily see that in the natural state there is nothing which by universal consent is good or evil, since everyone in a natural state consults only their own profit; deciding according to their own way of thinking what is good and what is evil with reference only to their own profit, and is not bound by any law to obey anyone but themselves.

Hence in a natural state *sin* cannot be conceived, but only in a civil state, where it is decided by universal consent what is good and what is evil, and where everyone is bound to obey the State. Sin, therefore, is nothing but *disobedience*, which is punished by the law of the State alone; obedience, on the other hand, being regarded as a merit in a citizen, because on account of it they are considered worthy to enjoy the privileges of the State.

Again, in a natural state no one by common consent is the owner of anything, nor is there anything in nature which can be said to be the rightful property of this and not of that person, but all things belong to all, so that in a natural state it is impossible to conceive a desire of rendering to each person their own or taking from another that which is their; that is to say, in a natural state there is nothing which can be called just or unjust, but only in a civil state, in which it is decided by universal consent what is one person's and what is another's.

Justice and injustice, therefore, sin and merit, are eternal notions and not attributes, which explain the nature of the mind. But enough of these matters.

PROP. 38. — *That which so disposes the human body that it can be affected in many ways, or which renders it capable of affecting external bodies in many ways, is profitable to a human being, and is more profitable in proportion as by its means the body becomes better fitted to be affected in many ways, and to affect other bodies; on the other hand, that thing is injurious which renders the body less fitted to affect or be affected.*

PROP. 39. — *Whatever is effective to preserve the proportion of motion and rest which the parts of the human body bear to each other is good, and, on the contrary, that is evil which causes the parts of the human body to have a different proportion of motion and rest to each other.*

Schol. — In what degree these things may injure or profit the mind will be explained in the Fifth Part. Here I observe merely that I understand the body to die when its parts are so disposed as to acquire a different proportion of motion and rest to each other. For I dare not deny that the human body, though the circulation of the blood and the other things by means of which it is thought to live be preserved, may, nevertheless, be changed into another nature altogether different from its own. No reason compels me to affirm that the body never dies unless it is changed into a corpse. Experience, indeed, seems to teach the contrary. It happens sometimes that a person undergoes such changes that he or she cannot very well be said to be the same person, as was the case with a certain Spanish poet of whom I have heard, who was seized with an illness, and although he or she recovered, remained, nevertheless, so oblivious of their past life that he or she did not believe the tales and tragedies he or she had composed were their own, and he or she might, indeed, have been taken for a grown-up child if he or she had also forgotten their native tongue.

But if this seems incredible, what shall we say of children? The person of mature years believes the nature of children to be so different from their own, that it would be impossible to persuade them that they had ever been a child, if they did not conjecture this being themselves from what they see of others. But in this matter, we avoid giving in to the superstitious matter for new reasons.

PROP 40. — *Whatever conduces to the universal fellowship of people, that is to say, whatever causes people to live in harmony with one another, is profitable, and on the contrary, whatever brings discord into the State is evil.*

PROP 41. — *Joy is not directly evil, but good; sorrow, on the other hand, is directly evil.*

PROP. 42. — *Cheerfulness can never be excessive but it's always good; melancholy, on the contrary, is always evil.*

PROP. 43. — *Pleasurable excitement may be excessive and an evil, and pain may be good, in so far as pleasurable excitement or joy is evil.*

PROP. 44. — *Love and desire may be excessive.*

Schol. — *Cheerfulness*, which I have affirmed to be good, is more easily imagined than observed; for the affects by which we are daily agitated are generally related to some part of the body which is affected more than the others, and therefore it is that the affects exist for the most part in excess, and so hold the mind down to the contemplation of one object alone, that it can think about nothing else; and although people are subject to a number of affects, and therefore few are found who are always under the control of one and the same affect, there are not wanting those to whom one and the same affect obstinately clings.

We see people sometimes so affected by one object, that although it is not present, they believe it to be before them; and if this happens to a person who is not asleep, we say that they are delirious or mad. Nor are those believed to be less mad who are inflamed by love, dreaming about nothing but a mistress or harlot day and night, for they excite our laughter. But the avaricious person who thinks of nothing else but gain or money, and the ambitious person who thinks of nothing: but glory, inasmuch as they do harm, and are, therefore, thought worthy of hatred, are not believed to be mad. In truth, however, avarice, ambition, lust, &c., are a kind of madness, although they are not reckoned amongst diseases.

PROP. 45. — *Hatred can never be good.*

Schol. — It is to be observed that here and in the following propositions I understand by hatred, hatred towards people only.

Corol. 1. — Envy, mockery, contempt, anger, revenge, and the other affects which are related to hatred or arise from it, are evil. This is also evident from Prop. 39 and 37.

Corol. 2. — Everything which we desire because we are affected by hatred is base and unjust in the State. This is also evident from Prop. 39 and 37 (what is base and unjust).

Schol. — I make a great distinction between *mockery* (which I have said is bad) and *laughter*; for laughter and merriment are nothing but joy, and therefore, provided they are not excessive, are in themselves good (Prop. 41). Nothing but a gloomy and sad superstition forbids enjoyment. For why is it more seemly to extinguish hunger and thirst than to drive away melancholy?

My reasons and my conclusions are these: — No God and no human being, except an envious one, is delighted by my impotence or my trouble, or esteems as any virtue in us tears, sighs, fears, and other things of this kind, which are signs of mental impotence; on the contrary, the greater the joy with which we are affected, the greater the perfection to which we pass thereby, that is to say, the more do we necessarily partake of the divine nature. To make use of things, therefore, and to delight in them as much as possible (provided we do not disgust ourselves with them, which is not delighting in them), is the part of a wise person.

It is the part of a wise person, I say, to refresh and invigorate themselves with moderate and pleasant eating and drinking, with sweet scents and the beauty of green plants, with ornament, with music, with sports, with the theatre, and with all things of this kind which one person can enjoy without hurting another.

For the human body is composed of a great number of parts of diverse nature, which constantly need new and varied nourishment, in order that the whole of the body may be equally fit for everything which can follow from its nature, and consequently that the mind may be equally fit to understand many things at once. This mode of living best of all agrees both with our principles and with common practice; therefore this mode of living is the best of all, and is to be universally commended There is no need, therefore, to enter more at length into the subject.

PROP. 46. — *People who live according to the guidance of reason strive as much as possible to repay the hatred, anger, or contempt of others towards themselves with love or generosity.*

Schol. — People who wish to avenge injuries by hating in return do indeed live miserably. But they who, on the contrary, strive to drive out hatred by love, fight joyfully and confidently, with equal ease resisting one person or a number of people, and needing scarcely any assistance from fortune. Those whom they conquer yield gladly, not from defect of strength, but from an increase of it. These truths, however, all follow so plainly from the definitions alone of love.

PROP. 47. — *The affects of hope and fear cannot be good of themselves.*

Schol. — We may here add that these affects indicate want of knowledge and impotence of mind, and, for the same reason, confidence, despair, gladness, and remorse are signs of weakness of mind. For although confidence and gladness are affects of joy, they nevertheless suppose that sorrow has preceded them, namely, hope or fear. In proportion, therefore, as we endeavour to live according to the guidance of reason, shall we strive as much as possible to depend less on hope, to liberate ourselves from fear, to rule fortune, and to direct our actions by the sure counsels of reason.

PROP. 48. — *The affects of over-estimation and contempt are always evil.*

PROP 49. — *Over-estimation easily renders the person who is over-estimated proud.*

PROP. 50. — *Pity in a person who lives according to the guidance of reason is in itself evil and unprofitable.*

Corol. — Hence it follows that a person who lives according to the dictates of reason endeavours as much as possible to prevent themselves from being touched by pity.

Schol. — The person who has properly understood that everything follows from the necessity of the divine nature, and comes to pass according to the eternal laws and rules of nature, will in truth discover nothing which is worthy of hatred, laughter, or contempt, nor will they pity any one, but, so far as human virtue is able, they will endeavour to *do well*, as we say, and to *rejoice.* We must add also, that people who are easily touched by the affect of pity, and are moved by the misery or tears of another, often do something of which they afterward repent, both because from an affect we do nothing which we certainly know to be good, and also because we are so easily deceived by false tears. But this I say expressly of the person who lives according to the guidance of reason. For a person who is moved neither by reason nor pity to be of any service to others is properly called inhuman; for (Prop. 27) this person seems to be unlike a human being.

PROP. 51. — *Favour is not opposed to reason, but agrees with it, and may arise from it.*

Schol. — Indignation, as it is defined by us (Def. 20 of the Affects), is necessarily evil (Prop. 45, pt. 4); but it is to be observed that when the supreme authority, constrained by the desire of preserving peace, punishes a citizen who injures another, I do not say that it is indignant with the citizen, since it is not excited by hatred to destroy them, but punishes them from motives of piety.

PROP. LII/52. — *Satisfaction may arise from reason, and the self-satisfaction alone which arises from reason is the highest which can exist.*

Corol. — Self-satisfaction is indeed the highest thing for which we can hope, for (as we have shown in Prop. 25, pt. 4) no one endeavours to preserve their being for the sake of any end. Again, because this self-satisfaction is more and more nourished and strengthened by praise (Corol. Prop. 53, pt. 3), and, on the contrary (Corol. Prop. 55, pt. 3), more and more disturbed by blame, therefore we are principally led by glory, and can scarcely endure life with disgrace.

PROP. 53. — *Humility is not a virtue, that is to say, it does not spring from reason.*

PROP. 54. — *Repentance is not a virtue that is to say, it does not spring from reason; on the contrary, the person who repents of what they have done is doubly wretched or impotent.*

Schol. — Inasmuch as people seldom live as reason dictates, therefore these two affects, humility and repentance, together with hope and fear, are productive of more profit than disadvantage, and therefore, since people must sin, it is better that they should sin in this way. For if men impotent in mind were all equally proud, were ashamed of nothing, and feared nothing, by what bonds could they be united or constrained? The multitude becomes a thing to be feared if it has nothing to fear. It is not to be wondered at, therefore, that the prophets, thinking rather of the good of the community than of a few, should have commended so greatly humility, repentance, and reverence. Indeed, those who are subject to these affects can be led much more easily than others, so that, at last, they come to live according to the guidance of reason, that is to say, become free human beings, and enjoy the life of the blessed.

PROP. 55.— *The greatest pride or the greatest despondence is the greatest ignorance of one's self.*

PROP. 56. — *The greatest pride or despondency indicates the greatest impotence of mind.*

Corol. — Hence follows, with the utmost clearness, that the proud and the desponding are above all others subject to affects.

Schol. — Despondency, nevertheless, can be corrected more easily than pride, since the former is an affect of sorrow, while the latter is an affect of joy, and is, therefore (Prop. 1S, pt, 4), stronger than the former.

PROP. 57. — *The proud person loves the presence of parasites or flatterers, and hates that of the noble-minded.*

Schol.— It would take too much time to enumerate here all the evils of pride, for the proud are subject to all affects, but to none are they less subject than to those of love and pity. It is necessary, however, to observe here that a person is also called proud if they think too little of other people, and so, in this sense, pride is to be defined as joy which arises from the false opinion that we are superior to other people, while despondency, the contrary o this pride, would be defined as sorrow arising from the false opinion that we are inferior to other people. This being understood, it is easy to see that the proud person is necessarily envious (Prop. 55), and that he or she hates those above all others who are the most praised on account of their virtues.

It follows, too, that their hatred of them is not easily overcome by love or kindness (Prop. 41), and that they are delighted by the presence of those only who humour their weakness, and from a fool make them a madman. Although despondency is contrary to pride, the despondent person is closely akin to the proud person. For since the sorrow of the despondent person arises from their judging their own impotence by the power or virtue of others, their sorrow will be mitigated, that is to say, they will rejoice, if their imagination be occupied in contemplating the vices of others. Hence the proverb —"It is a consolation to the wretched to have had companions in their misfortunes."

On the other hand, the more the despondent person believes themselves to be below other people, the more will he or she sorrow; and this is the reason why none are more prone to envy than the despondent; and why they, above all others, try to observe human actions with a view to finding fault with them rather than correcting them, so that at last they praise nothing but despondency and glory in it; but in such a manner, however, as always to seem despondent.

These things follow from this affect as necessarily as it follows from the nature of a triangle that its three angles are equal to two right angles. It is true, indeed, that I have said that I call these and the like affects evil, in so far as I attend to human profit alone; but the laws of nature have regard to the common order of nature of which person is a part — a remark I desired to make in passing, lest it should be thought that I talk about the vices and absurdities of people rather than attempt. to demonstrate the nature and properties of things. As I said in the Preface to the Third Part, I consider human affects and their properties precisely as I consider other natural objects; and, indeed, the affects of people, if they do not how their power, show, at least, the power and workmanship of nature, no less than many other things which we admire and delight to contemplate. I proceed, however, to notice those things connected with the affects which are productive either of profit or loss to human beings.

PROP. 58. — *Self-exaltation is not opposed to reason, but may spring from it.*

Schol. — What is called vainglory is self-satisfaction, nourished by nothing but the good opinion of the multitude, so that when that is withdrawn, the satisfaction, that is to say (Prop. 52), the chief good which everyone loves, ceases. For this reason those who glory in the good opinion of the multitude anxiously and with daily care strive, labour, and struggle to preserve their fame. For the multitude is changeable and fickle, so that fame, if it be not preserved, soon passes away. As everyone, moreover, is desirous to catch the praises of the people, one person will readily destroy the fame of another; and, consequently, as the object of contention is what is commonly thought to be the highest good, a great desire arises on the part of every one to keep down their fellows by every possible means, and the persons who at last come off as conquerors boast more because they have injured another person than because they have profited themselves.

This glory of self-satisfaction, therefore, is indeed vain, for it is really no glory. What is worthy of notice with regard to shame may easily be gathered from what has been said about compassion and repentance. I will only add that pity, like shame, although it is not a virtue, is nevertheless good, in so far as it shows that a desire of living uprightly is present in the person who is possessed with shame, just as pain is called good in so far as it shows that the injured part has not yet putrefied.

People, therefore, who are ashamed of what they have done, although they are sorrowful, are nevertheless more perfect than the shameless people who have no desire of living uprightly. These are the things which I undertook to establish with regard to the affects of joy and sorrow. With reference to the desires, these are good or evil as they spring from good or evil affects. All of them, however, in so far as they are begotten in us of affects which are passions, are blind nor would they be of any use if people could be easily persuaded to live according to the dictates of reason alone.

PROP. 59. — *To all actions to which we are determined by an affect which is a passion, we may without the affect, be determined by reason.*

Schol. — This can be explained more clearly by an example. The action of striking, for instance, in so far as it is considered physically, and we attend only to the fact that a person raises their arm, closes their hand, and forcibly moves the whole arm downwards, is a virtue which is conceived from the structure of the human body. If, therefore, a person agitated by anger or hatred is led to close the fist or move the arm, this comes to pass, as we have shown in the Second Part, because one and the same action can be joined to different images of things, and therefore we may be led to one and the same action as well by the images of things which we conceive confusedly as by those which we conceive clearly and distinctly. It appears, therefore, that every desire which arises from an affect which is a passion would be of no use if people could be led by reason. We shall now see why a desire which arises from an affect which is a passion is called blind.

PROP. 60. — *The desire which arises from joy or sorrow, which is related to one or to some, but not to all, the parts of the body, has no regard to the profit of the whole person.*

Schol. — Since, therefore, joy is most frequently related to one part of the body (Prop. 44), we generally desire to preserve our being without reference to our health as a whole; and moreover, the desires by which we are chiefly controlled (Prop. 9) have regard to the present only, and not to the future.

PROP. 61. — *A desire which springs from reason can never be in excess.*

PROP. 62. — *In so far as the conception of an object is formed by the mind according to the dictate of reason, the mind is equally affected, whether the idea be that of something future, past, or present.*

Schol. — If it were possible for us to possess an adequate knowledge concerning the duration of things, and to determine by reason the periods of their existence, we should contemplate with the same affect objects future and present, and the good which the mind conceived to be future, it would seek just as it would seek the present good. Consequently it would necessarily neglect the present good for the sake of a greater future good, and would, as we shall presently show, be very little disposed to seek a good which was present, but which would be a cause of any future evil.

But it is not possible for us to have any other than a very inadequate knowledge of the duration of things (Prop. 31), and we determine (Schol. Prop. 44) the periods of the existence of objects by the imagination alone, which is not affected by the image of a present object in the same way as it is by that of a future object. Hence it comes to pass that the true knowledge of good and evil which we possess is only abstract or universal, and the judgment we pass upon the order of things and the connection of causes, so that we may determine what s good for us in the present and what is evil, is rather imaginary than real. It is not, therefore, to be wondered at if the desire which arises from a knowledge of good and evil, in so far as this knowledge has regard to the future, is capable of being easily restrained by the desire of objects which are sweet to us at the present moment (Prop. 16)

PROP. 63. — People *who are led by fear and do what is good in order that they may avoid what is evil, are not led by reason.*

Schol. — The superstitious, who know better how to rail at vice than to teach virtue, and who study not to lead people by reason, but to hold them in through fear, in order that they may shun evil rather than love virtue, aim at nothing more than that others should be as miserable as themselves, and therefore, it is not to be wondered at if they generally become annoying and hateful to other people.

Corol. — By the desire which springs from reason we follow good directly and avoid evil indirectly.

Schol. — This is explained by the example of a sick person and a healthy person. The sick person, through fear of death, eats what he or she dislikes; the healthy persons take pleasure in their food, and so enjoys life more than if they feared death and directly desired to avoid it. So also the judge who condemns a guilty person to death, not from hatred or anger, but solely from love for the public welfare, is led by reason alone.

PROP. 64. — *The knowledge of evil is inadequate knowledge.*

Corol. — Hence it follows that if the human mind had none but adequate ideas, it would form no notion of evil.

PROP. 65. — *According to the guidance of reason, of two things which are good, we shall follow the greater good, and of two evils, we shall follow the less.*

Corol. — According to the guidance of reason, we shall follow a lesser evil for the sake of a greater good, and a lesser good which is the cause of a greater evil we shall neglect. For the evil which we here call less is really a good, and the good, on the other hand, is evil; and therefore (Prop. 63) we shall seek the former and neglect the latter.

PROP. 66. — *According to the guidance of reason, we shall seek the greater future good before that which is and present, and we shall seek also the less and present evil before that which is greater and future.*

Corol. — According to the guidance of reason, we shall seek the lesser present evil which is the cause of the greater future good, and the lesser present good which is the cause of a greater future evil we shall neglect.

Schol. — If what has been said here be compared with what has been demonstrated about the strength of the passions in the first eighteen Props, it will easily be seen in what consists the difference between people who are led by affect or opinion alone and those who are led by reason. The former, whether they will it or not, do those things of which they are entirely ignorant, but the latter do the will of no one but themselves, and do those things only which they know are of greatest importance in life, and which they therefore desire above all things. I call the former, therefore, *slaves*, and the latter *free*.

I will add here a few words concerning the character of the free person and their manner of life.

PROP. 67. — *A free person thinks of nothing less than of death and their wisdom is not a meditation upon death but upon life.*

PROP. 68. — *If people were born free they would form no conception of good and evil so long as they were free.*

Schol, — It is clear from Prop. 4, that the hypothesis of this proposition is false, and cannot be conceived unless in so far as we regard human nature alone, or rather God, not in so far as God is infinite, but in so far only as God is the cause of human existence. This (together with the other things we have before demonstrated) appears to have been what was meant by Moses in that history of the first man and woman. In that history no other power of God is conceived excepting that by which God created human beings; that is to say, the power with which God considered nothing but the advantage of humans.

Therefore we are told that God forbad free people to eat of the tree of knowledge of good and evil, and warned them that as soon as they ate of it they would immediately dread death rather than desire to live. Afterwards we are told that when man found a wife who agreed entirely with his nature, he saw that there could be nothing in nature which could be more profitable to him than his wife. But when he came to believe that the animals were like themselves, he immediately began to imitate their affects (Prop. 27), and to lose his liberty, which the Patriarchs afterwards recovered, being led by the spirit of Christ, that is to say, by the idea of God, which alone can make people free, and cause them to desire for other people the good they desire for themselves, as (Prop. 37) we have already demonstrated.

PROP. 69. — *The virtue of a free person is seen to be as great in avoiding danger as in overcoming it.*

Corol. — Flight at the proper time, just as well as fighting, is to be reckoned, therefore, as showing strength of mind in a person who is free; that is to say, a free person chooses flight by the same strength or presence of mind as that by which they choose battle.

Schol. — What strength of mind is, or what I understand by it, I have explained in Prop. 59. By danger, I understand anything which may be the cause of sorrow, hatred, discord, or any other evil like them.

PROP 70. — *The free person who lives amongst those who are ignorant strives as much as possible to avoid their favours.*

Schol. — I say as much as possible. For although people are ignorant, they are nevertheless people, who, when we are in straits, are able to afford us human assistance — the best assistance which a person can receive. It is often necessary, therefore, to receive a favour from the ignorant, and to thank them for it according to their taste; and besides this, care must be used, even in declining favours, not to seem either to despise the givers or through avarice to dread a return, so that we may not, while striving to escape their hatred, by that very act incur their displeasure. In avoiding favours, therefore, we must be guided by a consideration of what is profitable and honourable.

PROP. 71. — *None but those who are free are very useful to one another.*

Schol. — The gratitude to one another of people who are led by blind desire is generally a matter of business or a snare rather than gratitude. Ingratitude, it is to be observed, is not an affect It is nevertheless base, because it is generally a sign that a person is too much affected by hatred, anger, pride, or avarice. For he or she who through stupidity does not know how to return a gift is not ungrateful; and much less is he or she ungrateful who is not moved by the gifts of a harlot to serve her lust, nor by those of a thief to conceal their thefts, nor by any other gifts of a similar kind. On the contrary, a person shows that he or she possesses a steadfast mind if he does not suffer themselves to be enticed by any gifts to their own or the common ruin.

PROP. 72. — *A free person never acts deceitfully, but always honourably.*

Schol. — If it be asked whether, if a person by breach of faith could escape from the danger of instant death, reason does not counsel them, for the preservation of their being, to break faith; I reply in the same way, that if reason gives such counsel, she gives it to all people, and reason therefore generally counsels people to make no agreements for uniting their strength and possessing laws in common except deceitfully, that is to say, to have in reality no common laws, which is absurd.

PROP. 73. — *People who are guided by reason are freer in a State where they live according to the common laws than they are in solitude where they obey themselves alone.*

Schol. — These, and the like things which we have demonstrated concerning the true liberty of human beings, are related to fortitude, that is to say (Schol. Prop. 59, pt. 3), to strength of mind and generosity. Nor do I think it worthwhile to demonstrate here, one by one, all the properties of fortitude, and still less to show how its possessor can hate no one, be angry with no one, can neither envy, be indignant with, nor despise anybody, and can least of all be proud.

For all this, together with truths of a like kind which have to do with the true life and religion, are easily deduced from Props. 37 and 46, pt. 4, which show that hatred is to be overcome by love, and that everyone who is guided by reason desires for others the good which he or she seeks for themselves.

In addition, we must remember what we have already observed in Schol. Prop. 50, pt. 4, and in other places, that the brave person will consider above everything that all things follow from the necessity of the divine nature; and that, consequently, whatever they think injurious and evil, and, moreover, whatever seems to be impious, dreadful, unjust, or wicked, arises from this, that they conceive things in a disturbed, mutilated, and confused fashion.

For this reason, their chief effort is to conceive things as they are in themselves, and to remove the hindrances to true knowledge, such as hatred, anger, envy, derision, pride, and others of this kind which we have before noticed; and so they endeavour, as we have said, as much as possible to do well and rejoice. How far human virtue reaches in the attainment of these things, and what it can do, I shall show in the following part.

APPENDIX

My observations in this part concerning the true method of life have not been arranged so that they could be seen at a glance, but have been demonstrated here and there according as I could more easily deduce one from another. I have determined, therefore, here to collect them, and reduce them under principal heads.

1.
All our efforts or desires follow from the necessity of our nature in such a manner that they can be understood either through it alone

as their proximate cause, or in so far as we are a part of nature, which part cannot be adequately conceived through itself and without the other individuals.

2.
The desires which follow from our nature in such a manner that they can be understood through it alone, are those which are related to the mind, in so far as it is conceived to consist of adequate ideas. The remaining desires are not related to the mind, unless in so far as it conceives things inadequately, whose power and increase cannot be determined by human power, but by the power of objects which are without us. The first kind of desires, therefore, are properly called actions, but the latter passions; for the first always indicate our power, and the latter, on the contrary, indicate our impotence and imperfect knowledge.

3.
Our actions, that is to say, those desires which are determined by human power or reason, are always good; the others may be good as well as evil.

4.
It is therefore most profitable to us in life to make perfect the intellect or reason as far as possible, and in this one thing consists the highest happiness or blessedness of human beings; for blessedness is nothing but the peace of mind which springs from the intuitive knowledge of God, and to perfect the intellect is nothing but to understand God, together with the attributes and actions of God, which flow from the necessity of God's nature. The final aim, therefore, of a person who is guided by reason, that is to say, the chief desire by which he or she strives to govern all their other desires, is that by which they are led adequately to conceive themselves and all things which can be conceived by their intelligence.

5.
There is no rational life therefore, without intelligence, and things are good only in so far as they assist people to enjoy that life of the mind which is determined by intelligence. Those things alone, on the other hand, we call evil which hinder people from perfecting their reason in enjoying a rational life.

6.
But because all those things of which a human being is the efficient cause are necessarily good, it follows that no evil can happen to humans except from external causes, that is I to say, except in so far as they are a part of the whole of nature, whose laws human nature is compelled to obey— compelled also to accommodate themselves to this whole of nature in almost an infinite number of ways.

7.
It is impossible that a person should not be a part of nature and follow her common order; but if they be placed amongst individuals who agree with their nature, their power of action will by that very fact be assisted and supported. But if, on the contrary, they be placed amongst individuals who do not in the least agree with their nature, they will scarcely be able without great change on their part to accommodate themselves to them.

8.
Anything that exists in nature which we judge to be evil or able to hinder us from existing and enjoying a rational life, we are allowed to remove .from us in that way which seems the safest; and whatever, on the other hand, we judge to be good or to be profitable for the preservation of our being or the enjoyment of a rational life, we are permitted to take for our use and use in any way we may think proper; and absolutely, everyone is allowed by the highest right of nature to do that which he or she believes contributes to their own profit.

9.
Nothing, therefore, can agree better with the nature of any object than other individuals of the same kind, and so (see § 7) there is nothing more profitable to people for the preservation of their being and the enjoyment of a rational life than a person who is guided by reason. Again, since there is no single thing we know which is more excellent than a person who is guided by reason, it follows that there is nothing by which a person can better show how much skill and talent he or she possesses than by so educating people that at last they will live under the direct authority of reason.

10.
In so far as people are carried away by envy or any affect of hatred towards one another, so far are they contrary to one another, and consequently so much the more are they to be feared, as they have more power than other individuals of nature.

11.
Minds, nevertheless, are not conquered by arms, but by love and generosity.

12.
Above all things is it profitable to people to form communities and to unite themselves to one another by bonds which may make all of them as one person; and absolutely, it is profitable for them to do whatever may tend to strengthen their friendships.

13.
But to accomplish this skill and watchfulness are required; for people are changeable (those being very few who live according to the laws of reason), and nevertheless generally envious and more inclined to vengeance than pity. To bear with each, therefore, according to their disposition and to refrain from imitating their affect requires a singular power of mind. But those, on the contrary, who know how to revile humans, to denounce them rather than teach virtues, and not to strengthen human minds but to weaken them, are injurious both to themselves and others, so that many of them through an excess of impatience and a false zeal for religion prefer living with animals rather than amongst people; just as boys of youths, unable to endure with equanimity the rebukes of their parents, fly to the army, choosing the discomfort of war and the rule of a tyrant rather than the comforts of home and the admonitions of a father, suffering all kinds of burdens to be imposed upon them in order that they may revenge themselves upon their parents.

14.
Although, therefore, people generally determine everything by their pleasure, many more advantages than disadvantages arise from their common union. It is better, therefore, to endure with equanimity the injuries inflicted by them, and to apply our minds to those things which subserve concord and the establishment of friendship.

15.
The things which beget concord are those which are related to justice, integrity, and honour; for besides that which is unjust and injurious, people take ill also anything which is esteemed base, or that any one should despise the received customs of the State. But in order to win love, those things are chiefly necessary which have reference to religion and piety.

16.
Concord, moreover, is often produced by fear, but it is without good faith. It is to be observed, too, that fear arises from impotence of mind, and therefore is of no service to reason; nor is pity, although it seems to present an appearance of piety.

17.
Men also are conquered by liberality, especially those who have not the means wherewith to procure what is necessary for the support of life. But to assist every one "who is needy far surpasses the strength or profit of a private person, for the wealth of a private person is altogether insufficient to supply such wants. Besides, the power of any one person is too limited for them to be able to unite every one with themselves in friendship. The care, therefore, of the poor is incumbent on the whole of society and concerns only the general profit.

18.
In the receipt. of benefits and in returning thanks, care altogether different must be taken..

19.
The love of a harlot, that is to say, the lust of sexual intercourse, which arises from mere external form, and absolutely all love which recognises any other cause than the freedom of the mind, easily passes into hatred, unless, which is worse, it becomes a species of delirium, and thereby discord is cherished rather than concord.

20.
With regard to marriage, it is plain that it is in accordance with reason, if the desire of connection is engendered not merely by

external form, but by a love of begetting children and wisely educating them; and if, in addition, the love both of the husband and wife has for its cause not external form merely, but chiefly liberty of mind.

21.
Flattery, too, produces concord, but only by means of the disgraceful crime of slavery or perfidy; for there are none who are more taken by flattery than the proud who wish to be first and are not so.

22.
There is a false appearance of piety and religion in dejection; and although dejection is the opposite of pride, the humble dejected person is very near akin to the proud.

23.
Shame also contributes to concord, but only with regard to those matters which cannot be concealed. Shame, too, inasmuch as it is a kind of sorrow, does not belong to the service of reason.

24.
The remaining affects of sorrow which have people for their object are directly opposed to justice, integrity, honour, piety, and religion; and although indignation may seem to present an appearance of equity, yet there is no law where it is allowed to everyone to judge the deeds of another, and to vindicate their own or another's right.

25.
Affability, that is to say, the desire of pleasing people, which is determined by reason, is related to piety. But if affability arise from an affect, it is ambition or desire, by which people, generally under a false pretence of piety, excite discords and seditions. For they who desire to assist other people, either by advice or by deed, in order that they may together enjoy the highest good, will strive, above all things, to win their love, and not to draw them into admiration, so that a doctrine may be named after them, nor absolutely to give any occasion for envy. In common conversation, too, they will avoid referring to the vices of people, and will take care only sparingly to speak of human impotence, while he or she

will talk largely of human virtue or power, and of the way by which it may be made perfect, so that people being moved not by fear or aversion, but solely by the affect of joy, may endeavour as much as they can to live under the rule of reason.

26.
Excepting humans, we know no individual thing in nature in whose mind we can take pleasure, nor any thing which we can unite with ourselves by friendship or any kind of intercourse, and therefore the law of our own profit does not demand that we should preserve anything which exists in nature excepting people, but teaches us to preserve it or destroy it in accordance with its varied uses, or to adapt it to our own service in any way whatever.

27.
The profit which we derive from objects without us, over and above the experience and knowledge which we obtain because we observe them and change them from their existing forms into others, is chiefly the preservation of the body, and for this reason those objects are the most profitable to us which can feed and nourish the body, so that all its parts are able properly to perform their functions. For the more capable the body is of being affected in many ways, and affecting external bodies in many ways, the more capable of thinking is the mind (Props. 38 and 39).

But there seem to be very few things in nature of this kind, and it is consequently necessary for the requisite nourishment of the body to use many different kinds of food; for the human body is composed of a great number of parts of different nature, which need constant and varied food in order that the whole of the body may be equally adapted for all those things which can follow from its nature, and consequently that the mind also may be equally adapted to conceive many things.

28.
The strength of one person would scarcely suffice to obtain these things if people did not mutually assist one another. As money has presented us with an abstract of everything, it has come to pass that its image above every other usually occupies the mind of the multitude, because they can imagine hardly any kind of joy without the accompanying idea of money as its cause.

29.
This, however, is a vice only in those who seek money not from poverty or necessity, but because they have learnt the arts of gain, by which they keep up a grand appearance. As for the body itself, they feed it in accordance with custom, but sparingly, because they believe that they lose so much of their goods as they spend upon the preservation of their body. Those, however, who know the true use of money, and regulate the measure of wealth according to their needs, live contented with few things.

30.
Since, therefore, those things are good which help the parts of the body to perform their functions, and since joy consists in this, that the power of humans, in so far as they are made up of mind and body, is helped or increased, it follows that all those things which bring joy are good. But inasmuch as things do not work to this end — that they may affect us with joy — nor is their power of action guided in accordance with our profit, and finally, since joy is generally related chiefly to some one part of the body, it follows that generally the affects of joy (unless reason and watchfulness be present), and consequently the desires which are begotten from them, are excessive. It is to be added, that an affect causes us to put that thing first which is sweet to us in the present, and that we are not able to judge the future with an equal affect of the mind.

31.
Superstition, on the contrary, seems to affirm that what brings sorrow is good, and, on the contrary, that what brings joy is evil. But, as we have already said (Prop. 45), no one excepting an envious person is delighted at my impotence or disadvantage, for the greater the joy with which we are affected, the greater the perfection to which we pass, and consequently the more do we participate in the divine nature; nor can joy ever be evil which is controlled by a true consideration for our own profit. On the other hand, people who are led by fear, and do what is good that they may avoid what is evil, are not guided by reason.

32.
But human power is very limited, and is infinitely surpassed by the power of external causes, so that we do not possess an absolute

power to adapt. to our service the things which are without us. Nevertheless we shall bear with equanimity those things which happen to us contrary to what a consideration of our own profit demands, if we are conscious that we have performed our duty, that the power we have could not reach so far as to enable us to avoid those things, and that we are a part of the whole of nature, whose order we follow. If we clearly and distinctly understand this, the part of us which is determined by intelligence, that is to say, the better part of us, will be entirely satisfied therewith, and in that satisfaction will endeavour to persevere; for, in so far as we understand, we cannot desire anything excepting what is necessary, nor absolutely, can we be satisfied with anything but the truth. Therefore in so far as we understand these things properly will the efforts of the better part of us agree with the order of the whole of nature.

END OF THE FOURTH PART

ETHICS
AN OUTLINE

Fifth Part

OF THE POWER OF THE INTELLECT, OR OF HUMAN LIBERTY

OF THE POWER OF THE INTELLECT, OR OF HUMAN LIBERTY

PREFACE

I PASS at length to the other part of Ethics which concerns the method or way which leads to liberty. In this part, therefore, I shall treat of the power of reason, showing how much reason itself can control the affects, and then what is freedom of mind or blessedness. Thence we shall see how much stronger the wise person is than the ignorant. In what manner and in what way the intellect should be rendered perfect, and with what art the body is to be cared for in order that it may properly perform its functions, I have nothing to do with here; for the former belongs to logic, the latter to medicine. I shall occupy myself here, as I have said, solely with the power of the mind or of reason, first of all showing the extent and nature of the authority which it has over the affects in restraining them and governing them; for that we have not absolute authority over them we have already demonstrated.

The Stoics indeed thought that the affects depend absolutely on our will, and that we are absolutely masters over them; but they were driven, by the contradiction of experience, though not by their own principles, to confess that not a little practice and study are required in order to restrain and govern the affects. This one of them attempted to illustrate, if I remember rightly, by the example of two dogs, one of a domestic and the other of a hunting breed; for they were able by habit to make the house-dog hunt, and the hunting dog, on the contrary, to desist from running after hares.

To the Stoical opinion Descartes much inclines. God affirms that the soul or mind is united specially to a certain part of the brain called the pineal gland, which the mind by the mere exercise of the will is able to move in different ways, and by whose help the mind perceives all the movements which are excited in the body and external objects. This gland he affirms is suspended in the middle of the brain in such a manner that it can be moved by the least motion of the animal spirits. Again, he affirms that any variation in the manner in which the animal spirits impinge upon this gland is followed by a variation in the manner in which it is suspended in the middle of the brain, and moreover that the number of different impressions on the gland is the same as that of the different external objects which propel the animal spirits towards it. Hence it comes to pass that if the gland, by the will of the soul moving it in different directions, be afterwards suspended in this or that way in which it had once been suspended by the spirits agitated in this or that way, then the gland itself will propel and determine the animal spirits themselves in the same way as that in which they had before been repelled by a similar suspension of the gland.

Moreover, he affirmed that each volition of the mind is united in nature to a certain motion of the gland. For example, if a person wishes to behold a remote object, this volition will cause the pupil of the eye to dilate, but if he thinks merely of the dilation of the pupil, to have that volition will profit them nothing, because nature has not connected a motion of the gland which serves to impel the animal spirits towards the optic nerve in a way suitable for dilation or contraction of the pupil with the volition of dilation or contraction, but only with the volition of beholding objects afar off or close at hand. Finally, he maintained that although each motion of this gland appears to be connected by nature from the commencement of our life with an individual thought, these motions can nevertheless be connected by habit with other thoughts, a proposition which he attempts to demonstrate in their "Passions of the Soul," art 50, pt. 1.

From this he concludes that there is no mind so feeble that it cannot, when properly directed, acquire absolute power over its passions; for passions, as defined by them, are "perceptions, or sensations, or emotions of the soul which are related to it specially, and which are produced, preserved, and strengthened by some motion of the spirits." (See the " Passions of the Soul," art. 27, pt. 1.)

But since it is possible to join to a certain volition any motion of the gland, and consequently of the spirits, and since the determination of the will depends solely on our power, we shall be able to acquire absolute mastery over our passions provided only we determine our will by fixed and firm decisions by which we desire to direct our actions and bind with these decisions the movements of the passions we wish to have. So far as I can gather from their own words, this is the opinion of that distinguished person, and I could scarcely have believed it possible for one so great to have put it forward if it had been less subtle.

I can hardly wonder enough that a philosopher who firmly resolved to make no deduction except. from self-evident principles, and to affirm nothing but what he clearly and distinctly perceived, and who blamed all the schoolmen because they desired to explain obscure matters by occult qualities, should accept. a hypothesis more occult than any occult quality. What does he understand, I ask, by the union of the mind and body? What clear and distinct conception has he of thought intimately connected with a certain small portion of matter? I wish that he had explained this union by its proximate cause. But he conceived the mind to be so distinct from the body that they were able to assign no single cause of this union, nor of the mind itself, but was obliged to have recourse to the cause of the whole universe, that is to say, to God.

Again, I should like to know how many degrees of motion the mind can give to that pineal gland, and with how great a power the mind can hold it suspended. For I do not understand whether this gland is acted on by the mind more slowly or more quickly than by the animal spirits, and whether the movements of the passions, which we have so closely bound with firm decisions, might not be separated from them again by bodily causes, from which it would follow that although the mind had firmly determined to meet danger, and had joined to this decision the motion of boldness, the sight of the danger might cause the gland to be suspended in such a manner that the mind could think of nothing, but flight.

Indeed, since there is no relation between the will and motion, so there is no comparison between the power or strength of the body and that of the mind, and consequently the strength of the body can never be determined by the strength of the mind. It is to be remembered also that this gland is not found to be so situated in the middle of the brain that it can be driven about so easily and in so many ways, and that all the nerves are not extended to the cavities of the brain.

Lastly, I omit all that Descartes asserts concerning the will and the freedom of the will, since I have shown over and over again that it is false. Therefore, inasmuch as the power of the mind, as I have shown above, is determined by intelligence alone, we shall determine by the knowledge of the mind alone the remedies against the affects — remedies which every one, I believe, has experienced, although there may not have been any accurate observation or distinct perception of them, and from this knowledge of the mind alone shall we deduce everything which relates to its blessedness.

AXIOM

1. If two contrary actions be excited in the same subject, a change must necessarily take place in both, or in one alone, until they cease to be contrary.

2. The power of an affect is limited by the power of its cause, in so far as the essence of the affect is explained or limited by the essence of the cause itself.

This axiom is evident from Prop. 7, pt. 3.

PROP. 1. — *As thoughts and the ideas of things are arranged and connected in the mind, exactly so are the affections of the body or the images of things arranged and connected in the body.*

PROP. 2. — *If we detach an emotion of the mind or affect from the thought of an external cause and connect it with other thoughts, then the love or hatred towards the external cause and the fluctuations of the mind which arise from these affects will be destroyed.*

PROP. 3. — *An affect which is a passion ceases to be a passion as soon as we form a dear and distinct idea of it.*

Corol. — In proportion, then, as we know an affect better is it more within our control, and the less does the mind suffer from it.

PROP. 4. — *There is no affection of the body of which we cannot form some dear and distinct conception.*

Corol. — Hence it follows that there is no affect of which we cannot form some clear and distinct conception. For an affect is an idea of an affection of the body (by the general definition of the Affects), and this idea therefore (Prop. 4, pt. 5) must involve some clear and distinct conception.

Schol. — Since nothing exists from which some effect does not follow (Prop. 36), and since we understand clearly and distinctly everything which follows from an idea which is adequate in us (Prop. 40), it is a necessary consequence that everyone has the power, partly at least, if not absolutely, of understanding clearly and distinctly themselves and their affects, and consequently of bringing it to pass that he or she suffers less from them. We have therefore mainly to strive to acquire a clear and distinct knowledge as far as possible of each affect so that the mind may be led to pass from the affect to think those things which it perceives clearly and distinctly, and with which it is entirely satisfied, and to strive also that the affect may be separated from the thought of a external cause and connected with true thoughts. Thus not only love, hatred, &c., will be destroyed (Prop. 2), but also the appetites or desires to which the affect gives rise cannot be excessive (Prop. 61). For it is above everything to be observed that the appetite by which a person is said to act is one and the same appetite as that by which they are said to suffer.

For example, we have shown that human nature is so constituted that every one desires that other people should live according to their way of thinking (Prop. 31), a desire which in a person who is not guided by reason is a passion which is called ambition, and is not very different from pride; while, on the other hand, in a person who lives according to the dictates of reason it is an action or virtue which is called piety (Prop. 37). In the same manner, all the appetites or desires are passions only in so far as they arise from inadequate ideas, and are classed among the virtues whenever they are excited or begotten by adequate ideas; for all the desires by which we are determined to any action may arise either from adequate or inadequate ideas (Prop. 59). To return, therefore, to the point from which we set out; there is no remedy within our power which can be conceived more excellent for the affects than that which consists in a true knowledge of them, since the mind possesses no other power than that of thinking and forming adequate ideas, as we have shown above (Prop. 3).

PROP 5. — *An affect towards an object which we do not imagine as necessary, possible, or contingent, but which we simply imagine, is, other things being equal, the greatest of all.*

PROP. 6. — *In so far as the mind understands all things as necessary, so far has it greater power over the affects, or suffers less from them.*

Schol. — The more this knowledge that things are necessary is applied to individual things which we imagine more distinctly and more vividly, the greater is this power of the mind over the affects, — a fact to which experience also testifies. For we see that sorrow for the loss of anything good is diminished if the person who has lost it considers that it could not by any possibility have been preserved. So also we see that nobody pities an infant because it does not know how to speak, walk, or reason, and lives so many years not conscious, as it were, of itself. But if a number of human beings were born adult, and only a few here and there were born infants, everyone would pity the infants, because we should then consider infancy not as a thing natural and necessary, but as a defect or fault of nature. Many other facts of a similar kind we might observe.

PROP. 7. — *The affects which spring from reason or which are excited by it are if time he or she taken into account, more powerful than those which are related to individual objects which we contemplate as absent.*

PROP. 8. — *The greater the number of the causes which simultaneously concur to excite any affect the greater it will be.*

PROP. 9. — *If we are affected by an affect which is related to many and different causes, which the mind contemplates at the same time with the affect itself we are less injured, suffer less from it, and are less affected therefore towards each cause than if we were affected* by another affect equally great which is related to one cause only or to fewer causes.

PROP. 10. — *So long as we are not agitated by affects which are contrary to our nature do we possess the power of arranging and connecting the affections of the body according to the order of the intellect.*

Schol. — Through this power of properly arranging and connecting the affections of the body, we can prevent ourselves from being easily affected by evil affects. For (Prop. 7, pt. 5) a greater power is required to restrain affects which are arranged and connected according to the order of the intellect than is required to restrain those which are uncertain and unsettled. The best thing, therefore, we can do, so long as we lack a perfect knowledge of our affects, is to conceive a right rule of life, or sure maxims (dogmata) of life, — to commit these latter to memory, and constantly to apply them to the particular cases which frequently meet us in life, so that our imagination may be widely affected by them, and they may always be ready to hand. For example, amongst the maxims of life we have placed this (see Prop. 46, pt. 4, with its Schol.), that hatred is to be conquered by love or generosity, and is not to be met with hatred in return.

But in order that we may always have this prescript of reason in readiness whenever it will be of service, we must think over and often meditate upon the common injuries inflicted by people, and consider how and in what way they may best be repelled by generosity; for thus we shall connect the image of injury with the imagination of this maxim, and (Prop. 18) it will be at hand whenever an injury is offered to us. If we also have at hand the law of our own true profit and good which follows from mutual friendship and common fellowship, and remember that the highest peace of mind arises from a right rule of life (Prop. 52), and also that man, like other things, acts according to the necessity of nature, then the injury or the hatred which usually arises from that necessity will occupy but the least part of the imagination, and will be easily overcome: or supposing that the anger which generally arises from the greatest injuries is not so easily overcome, it will nevertheless be overcome, although not without fluctuation of mind, in a far shorter space of time than would have been necessary if we had not possessed those maxims on which we had thus meditated beforehand. This is evident from Props. 6, 7, and 8.

Concerning strength of mind, we must reflect in the same way for the purpose of getting rid of fear, that is to say, we must often enumerate and imagine the common dangers of life, and think upon the manner in which they can best be avoided and overcome by presence of mind and courage. It is to be observed, however, that in the ordering of our thoughts and images we must always look (Props. 63 and 59) to those qualities which in each thing are good, so that we may be determined to action always by an affect of joy.

For example, if a person sees that he or she pursues glory too eagerly, let them think on its proper use, for what end it is to be followed, and by what means it can be obtained; but let them not think upon its abuse and vanity, and on the inconstancy of people and things of this sort, about which no one thinks unless through disease of mind; for with such thoughts do those who are ambitious greatly torment themselves when they despair of obtaining the honours for which they are striving; and while they vomit forth rage, wish to be thought wise. Indeed it is certain that those covet glory the most who are loudest in declaiming against its abuse and the vanity of the world.

Nor is this a peculiarity of the ambitious, but is common to all to whom fortune is adverse and who are impotent in mind; for we see that a poor and avaricious person is never weary of speaking about the abuse of money and the vices of the rich, thereby achieving nothing save to torment themselves and show to others that they are unable to bear with equanimity not only their own poverty but also the wealth of others. So also a person who has not been well received by their mistress thinks of nothing but the fickleness of women, their faithlessness, and their other oft-proclaimed failings, — all of which he or she forgets as soon as they are taken into favour by their mistress again.

He, therefore, who desires to govern their affects and appetites from a love of liberty alone will strive as much as he or she can to know virtues and their causes, and to fill their mind with that joy which springs from a true knowledge of them. Least of all will he or she desire to contemplate the vices of people and disparage people, or to delight in a false show of liberty. God who will diligently observe these things (and they are not difficult), and will continue to practise them, will assuredly in a short space of time be able for the most part to direct their actions in accordance with the command of reason.

PROP. 11. — *The greater the number of objects to which an image is related, the more constant is it, or the more frequently does it present itself and the more does it occupy the mind.*

PROP. 12. — *The images of things are more easily connected with those images which are related to things which we clearly and distinctly underhand than with any others.*

PROP. 13. — *The greater the number of other things with which any image is connected, the more frequently does it present itself.*

PROP. 14. — *The mind can cause all the affections of the body or the images of things to be related to the idea of God (idea Dei).*

PROP. 15. — *God who clearly and distinctly understands themselves and their affects loves God, and loves God better the better he or she understands themselves and their affects.*

PROP. 16. — *This love to God above everything else ought to occupy the mind.*

PROP. 17. — *God is free from passions, nor is God affected with any affect of joy or sorrow.*

Corol.— Properly speaking, God loves no one and hates no one; for God (Prop. 17) is not affected with any affect of joy or sorrow, and consequently (Defs. 6 and 7 of the Affects) God neither loves nor hates any one.

PROP. 18. — *No one can hate God.*

Corol. — Love to God cannot be turned into hatred.

Schol. — But some may object, that if we understand God to be the cause of all things, we do for that very reason consider God to be the cause of sorrow. But I reply, that in so far as we understand the causes of sorrow, it ceases to be a passion (Prop. 3), that is to say (Prop. 59), it ceases to be sorrow; and therefore in so far as we understand God to be the cause of sorrow do we rejoice.

PROP. 19. — God *who loves God cannot strive that God should love them in return.*

PROP. 20. — *This love to God cannot be defiled either by the affect of envy or jealousy, but is the more strengthened the more people we imagine to be connected with God by the same bond of love.*
affect directly contrary to this love and able to destroy it, and so we may conclude that this love to God is the most constant of all the affects, and that, in so far as it is related to the body, it cannot be destroyed unless with the body itself. What its nature is, in so far as it is related to the mind alone, we shall see hereafter.

I have, in what has preceded, included all the remedies for the affects, that is to say, everything which the mind, considered in itself alone, can do against them It appears there from that the power of the mind over the affects consists —

1. In the knowledge itself of the affects. (See Schol. Prop. 4, pt. 5.)

2. In the separation by the mind of the affects from the thought of an external cause, which we imagine confusedly. (See Prop. 2, pt. 5, and Schol. Prop. 4, pt. 5.)

3. In duration, in which the affections which are related to objects we understand surpass those related to objects conceived in a mutilated or confused manner. (Prop. 7, pt. 5.)

4. In the multitude of causes by which the affections which are related to the common properties of things or to God are nourished. (Props. 9 and 1 1, pt. 5.)

5. In the order in which the mind can arrange its affects and connect them one with the other. (Schol. Prop. 10, pt. 5, and see also Props. 12, 13, and 14, pt. 5.)

But that this power of the mind over the affects may be better understood, it is to be carefully observed that we call the affects great when we compare the affect of one person with that of another, and see that one person is agitated more than another by the same affect, or when we compare the affects of one and the same person with one another, and discover that they are affected or moved more by one affect than by another. For (Prop. 5, pt. 4) the power of any affect is limited by the power of the external cause as compared with our own power. But the power of the mind is limited solely by knowledge, whilst impotence or passion is estimated solely by privation of knowledge, or, in other words, by that through which ideas are called inadequate; and it therefore follows that that mind suffers the most whose largest part consists of inadequate ideas, so that it is distinguished rather by what it suffers than by what it does, while, on the contrary, that mind acts the most whose largest part consists of adequate ideas, so that although it may possess as many inadequate ideas as the first, it is nevertheless distinguished rather by those which belong to human virtue than by those which are a sign of human impotence.

Again, it is to be observed that our sorrows and misfortunes mainly proceed from too much love towards an object which is subject to many changes, and which we can never possess. For no one is troubled or anxious about any object he or she does not love, neither do wrongs, suspicions, hatreds, &c., arise except. from love towards objects of which no one can be truly the possessor.

From all this we easily conceive what is the power which clear and distinct knowledge, and especially that third kind of knowledge (see Prop. 47) whose foundation is the knowledge itself of God, possesses over the affects; the power, namely, by which it is able, in so far as they are passions, if not actually to destroy them (see Prop. 3, 4), at least to make them constitute the smallest part of the mind (Prop. 14, pt. 5). Moreover, it begets a love towards an immutable and eternal object (Prop. 45, pt. 5) of which we are really partakers (Prop 45, pt. 2); a love which therefore cannot be vitiated by the defects which are in common love, but which can always become greater and greater (Prop. 15, pt. 5), occupy the largest part of the mind (Prop. 16, pt. 5), and thoroughly affect it.

I have now concluded all that I had to say relating to this present life. For anyone who will attend to what has been urged in this scholium, and to the definition of the mind and its affects, and to Props. 1 and 3, pt. 3, will easily be able to see the truth of what I said in the beginning of the scholium, that in these few words all the remedies for the affects are comprehended. It is time, therefore, that I should now pass to the consideration of those matters which appertain to the duration of the mind without relation to the body.

PROP. 21. — *The mind can imagine nothing, or can it recollect anything that is past, except. while the body exists.*

PROP. 22. — *In God, nevertheless there necessarily exists an idea which expresses the essence of this or that human body under the form of eternity.*

PROP. 23.—*The human mind cannot be absolutely destroyed with the body, but something of it remains which is eternal.*

Schol. — This idea which expresses the essence of the body under the form of eternity is, as we have said, a certain mode of thought which pertains to the essence of the mind, and is necessarily eternal. It is impossible, nevertheless, that we should recollect that we existed before the body, because there are no traces of any such existence in the body, and also because eternity cannot be defined by time, or have any relationship to it Nevertheless we feel and know by experience that we are eternal. For the mind is no less sensible of those things which it conceives through intelligence than of those which it remembers, for demonstrations are the eyes of the mind by which it sees and observes things.

Although, therefore, we do not recollect that we existed before the body, we feel that our mind, in so far as it involves the essence of the body under the form of eternity, is eternal, and that this existence of the mind cannot be limited by time nor explained by duration. Only in so far, therefore, as it involves the actual existence of the body can the mind be said to possess duration, and its existence be limited by a fixed time, and so far only has it the power of determining the existence of things in time, and of conceiving them under the form of duration.

PROP. 24. — *The more we understand individual objects, the more we understand God.*

PROP. 25. — *The highest effort of the mind and its highest virtue is to understand things by the third kind of knowledge.*

PROP. 26. — *This letter the mind is adapted to understand things by the third kind of knowledge, the more it desires to understand them by this kind of knowledge.*

PROP. 27. — *From this third kind of knowledge arises the highest possible peace of mind.*

PROP. 28. — *The effort or the desire to know things by the third kind of knowledge cannot arise from the first kind, but may arise from the second kind of knowledge.*

PROP. 29. — *Everything which the mind understands under the form of eternity it understands not because it conceives the present actual existence of the body, but because it conceives the essence of the body under the form of eternity.*

Schol. — Things are conceived by us as actual in two ways; either in so far as we conceive them to exist with relation to a fixed time and place, or in so far as we conceive them to be contained in God, and to follow from the necessity of the divine nature. But those things which are conceived in this second way as true or real we conceive under the form of eternity, and their ideas involve the eternal and infinite essence of God, as we have shown in Prop. 45, pt. 2.

PROP. 30. — *Our mind, in so far as it knows itself and the body under the form of eternity, necessarily has knowledge of God, and knows that it is in God and is conceived through God.*

PROP. 31. — *The third kind of knowledge depends upon the mind as its formal cause, in so far as the mind itself is eternal.*
Schol. — As each person therefore becomes stronger in this kind of knowledge, the more is he or she conscious of themselves and of God; that is to say, the more perfect and the happier they are, a truth which will still more clearly appear from what follows. Here, however, it is to be observed, that although we are now certain that

the mind is eternal in so far as it conceives things under the form of eternity, yet, in order that what we wish to prove may be more easily explained and better understood, we shall consider the mind, as we have hitherto done, as if it had just begun to be, and had just begun to understand things under the form of eternity. This we can do without any risk of error, provided only we are careful to conclude nothing except. from clear premises.

PROP. 32. — *In whatever we understand by the third kind of knowledge we delight and our delight is accompanied with the idea of God as its cause.*

Corol. — From the third kind .of knowledge necessarily springs the intellectual love of God. For from this kind of knowledge arises (Prop. 32, pt. 5) joy attended with the idea of God as its cause, that is to say (Def. 6 of the Affects), the love of God, not in so far as we imagine God as present (Prop. 29, pt. 5), but in so far as we understand that God is eternal; and that is what I call the intellectual love of God.

PROP. 33. — *The intellectual love of God which arises from the third hind of knowledge is eternal.*

PROP. 34. — *The mind is subject to affects which are related to passions only so long as the body exists.*

Corol. — Hence it follows that no love except intellectual love is eternal.

Schol. — If we look at the common opinion of people, we shall see that they are indeed conscious of the eternity of their minds, but they confound it with duration, and attribute it to imagination or memory, which they believe remain after death.

PROP. 35. — *God loves Godself with an infinite intellectual love.*

Corol. — Hence it follows that God, in so far as God loves Godself, loves people, and consequently that the love of God towards people and the intellectual love of the mind towards God are one and the same thing.

Schol, — Hence we clearly understand that our salvation, or blessedness, or liberty consists in a constant and eternal love towards God, or in the love of God towards people. This love or blessedness is called Glory in the sacred writings, and not without reason. For whether it be related to God or to the mind, it may properly be called repose of mind, which (Defs. 25 and 30 of the Affects) is, in truth, not distinguished from glory. For in so far as it is related to God, it is (Prop. 35, pt. 5) joy (granting that it is allowable to use this word), accompanied with the idea of Godself, and it is the same thing when it is related to the mind (Prop. 27, pt. 5). Again, since the essence of our mind consists in knowledge alone, whose beginning and foundation is God (Prop. 15, pt. 1, and Prop. 47, pt. 2), it is clear to us in what manner and by what method our mind, with regard both to essence and existence, follows from the divine nature, and continually depends upon God. I thought it worthwhile for me to notice this here, in order that I might show, by this example, what that knowledge of individual objects which I have called intuitive or of the third kind (Schol. 2, Prop. 40, pt. 2) is able to do, and how much more potent it is than the universal knowledge, which I have called knowledge of the second kind. For although I have shown generally in the First Part that all things, and consequently also the human mind, depend upon God both with regard to existence and essence, yet that demonstration, although legitimate, and placed beyond the possibility of a doubt, does not, nevertheless, so affect our mind as a proof from the essence itself of any individual object which we say depends upon God.

PROP. 37. — Here *is nothing in nature which is contrary to this intellectual love, or which can negate it.*

PROP. 38. — *The more objects the mind understands by the second and third hinds of knowledge, the less it suffers from those affects which are evil, and the less it fears death.*

Schol. — We are thus enabled to understand that which I touched upon in Schol. Prop. 39, pt. 4, and which I promised to explain in this part, namely, that death is by so much the less injurious to us as the clear and distinct knowledge of the mind is greater, and consequently as the mind loves God more. Again, since (Prop. 27, pt. 5) from the third kind of knowledge there arises the highest possible peace, it follows that it is possible for the human mind to be of such a nature that that part of it which we have shown perishes with its body (Prop. 21, pt. s), in comparison with the part of it which remains, is of no consequence. But more fully upon this subject presently.

PROP. 39. — *A person who possesses a body fit for many things possesses a mind of which the greater part is eternal.*

Schol. — Inasmuch as human bodies are fit for many things, we cannot doubt the possibility of their possessing such a nature that they may be related to minds which have a large knowledge of themselves and of God, and whose greatest or principal part is eternal, so that they scarcely fear death. To understand this more clearly, it is to be here considered that we live in constant change, and that according as we change for the better or the worse we are called happy or unhappy. For he or she who passes from infancy or childhood to death is called unhappy, and, on the other hand, we consider ourselves happy, if we can pass through the whole period of life with a sound mind in a sound body. Moreover, he or she who, like an infant or child, possesses a body fit for very few things, and almost altogether dependent on external causes, has a mind which, considered in itself alone, is almost entirely unconscious of itself, of God, and of objects. On the other hand, he or she who possesses a body fit for many things possesses a mind which, considered in itself alone, is largely conscious of itself, of God, and of objects. In this life therefore, it is our chief endeavour to change the body of infancy, so far as its nature permits and is conducive thereto, into another body which is fitted for many things, and which is related to a mind conscious as much as possible of itself, of God, and of objects; so that everything which is related to its memory or imagination, in comparison with the intellect is scarcely of any moment, as I have already said in the scholium of the preceding proposition.

PROP. 40. — *The more perfection a thing possesses, the more it acts and the less it suffers, and conversely the more it acts the more perfect it is.*

whether great or small, is more perfect than the other part. For the part of the mind which is eternal (Props. 23 and 29, pt. 5) is the intellect, through which alone we are said to act (Prop. 1, pt. 3), but that part which, as we have shown, perishes, is the imagination itself (Prop. 21, pt. S), through which alone we are said to suffer (Prop. 3, pt. 3, and the general definition of the Affects). Therefore (Prop. 40, pt. 5) that part which abides, whether great or small, is more perfect than the latter. — Q.E.D.

Schol. — These are the things I proposed to prove concerning the mind, in so far as it is considered without relation to the existence of the body, and from these, taken together with Prop. 21, pt. 1, and other propositions, it is evident that our mind, in so far as it understands, is an eternal mode of thought, which is determined by another eternal mode of thought, and this again by another, and so on *ad infinitum*, so that all taken together form the eternal and infinite intellect of God.

PROP. 41. — *Even if we did not know that our mind is eternal, we should still consider as of primary importance Piety and Religion, and absolutely everything which in the Fourth Part we have shown to be related to strength of mind and generosity,*

Schol. — The creed of the multitude seems to be different from this; for most persons seem to believe that they are free in so far as it is allowed them to obey their lusts, and that they give up a portion of their rights, in so far as they are bound to live according to the commands of divine law. Piety, therefore, and religion, and absolutely all those things that are related to greatness of soul, they believe to be burdens which they hope to be able to lay aside after death; hoping also to receive some reward for their bondage, that is to say, for their piety and religion. It is not merely this hope, however, but also and chiefly fear of dreadful punishments after death, by which they are induced to live according to the commands of divine law, that is to say, as far as their feebleness and impotent mind will permit; and if this hope and fear were not present to them, but if they, on the contrary, believed that minds perish with the body, and that there is no prolongation of life for miserable creatures exhausted with the burden of their piety, they would return to ways of their own liking; they would prefer to let everything be controlled by their own passions, and to obey fortune rather than themselves.

This seems to me as absurd as if a person, because he or she does not believe that he or she will be able to feed their body with good food to all eternity, should desire to satiate themselves with poisonous and deadly drugs; or as if, because he or she sees that the mind is not eternal or immortal, he or she should therefore prefer to be mad and to live without reason, — absurdities so great that they scarcely deserve to be repeated.

PROP. XLII/42. — *Blessedness is not the reward of virtue, but is virtue itself; nor do we delight in blessedness because we restrain our lusts; but, on the contrary, because we delight in it, therefore are we able to restrain them.*

Again, the more the mind delights in this divine love or blessedness, the more it understands (Prop. 32, pt. 5), that is to say (Corol. Prop. 3, pt. 5), the greater is the power it has over its affects, and (Prop. 38, pt. 5) the less it suffers from affects which are evil. Therefore, it is because the mind delights in this divine love or blessedness that it possesses the power of restraining the lusts; and because the power of human beings to restrain the affects is in the intellect alone, no one, therefore, delights in blessedness because they have restrained their affects, but, on the contrary, the power of restraining their lusts springs from blessedness itself. — Q.E.D.

Schol. — I have finished everything I wished to explain concerning the power of the mind over the affects and concerning its liberty. From what has been said we see 'hat is the strength of the wise person, and how much he or she surpasses the ignorant who is driven forward by lust alone. For the ignorant person is not only agitated by external causes in many ways, and never enjoys true peace of soul, but lives also ignorant, as it were, both of God and of things, and as soon as he or she ceases to suffer ceases also to be. On the other hand, the wise person, in so far as they are considered as such, is scarcely ever moved in their mind, but, being conscious by a certain eternal necessity of themselves, of God, and of things, never ceases to be, and always enjoys true peace of soul. If the way which, as I have shown, leads hither seem very difficult, it can nevertheless be found. It must indeed be difficult since it is so seldom discovered; for if salvation lay ready to hand and could be discovered without great labour, how could it be possible that it should be neglected almost by everybody? But all noble things are as difficult as they are rare.

FINIS

www.ingramcontent.com/pod-product-compliance
Lightning Source LLC
Chambersburg PA
CBHW051803040426
42446CB00007B/485